Reading

Mentor
joy
START 3

Longman
Reading Mentor joy START ❸

지은이 교재개발연구소
편집 및 기획 English Nine
발행처 Pearson Education South Asia Pte Ltd.
판매처 inkedu(inkbooks)
전화 02-455-9620(주문 및 고객지원)
팩스 02-455-9619
등록 제13-579호

ISBN 979-11-88228-34-8

잘못된 책은 구입처에서 바꿔 드립니다.

Longman

Reading

Mentor

joy

START 3

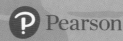
Pearson

Introduction

Reading Mentor Joy Start 시리즈는 초등학생 및 초보자를 위한 영어 읽기 학습 교재로, 전체 2개의 레벨 총 6권으로 구성되어 있습니다.

이 시리즈는 수준별로 다양한 주제의 글들을 통해서 학습자들의 문장 이해력과 글 독해력 향상을 주요 목표로 하고 있습니다. 또한 어휘와 문맥을 파악하고 글의 특성에 맞는 글 독해력 향상을 위한 체계적인 코너들을 구성하여 전체 내용을 효과적으로 이해할 수 있도록 구성했습니다.

학습자들의 수준에 맞는 다양한 주제의 글들을 통해서 학습에 동기부여를 제공함과 더불어 다양한 배경 지식과 상식을 넓히는 계기가 될 것입니다.

Reading Mentor **joy** START

Book 1	Book 2	Book 3

Reading Mentor **joy**

Book 1	Book 2	Book 3

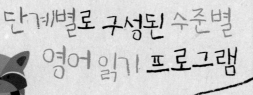

단계별로 구성된 수준별
영어 읽기 프로그램

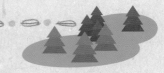

- 흥미 있는 토픽별 읽을거리
- 문맥을 통한 내용 파악 연습
- 재미있게 영단어 확인 학습
- 스토리 속 숨어 있는 문법 학습
- 다양한 학습 능력을 활용한 문제 구성

Reading Mentor Joy Start 스토리 소개

Book	Chapter
START 1	1 **Animals** 동물
	2 **Friends** 친구
	3 **Hobby** 취미
	4 **Jobs** 직업
	5 **Family** 가족
	6 **Places** 장소
START 2	1 **School Life** 학교 생활
	2 **Favorite Things** 좋아하는 것들
	3 **Nature** 자연
	4 **Daily Life** 일상생활
	5 **Visiting the Doctor** 의사 방문하기
	6 **Introducing Yourself** 자기소개 하기
START 3	1 **Clothes** 옷
	2 **Sports** 스포츠
	3 **Seasons and Weather** 계절과 날씨
	4 **Pets** 애완동물
	5 **In the Woods** 숲에서
	6 **Health** 건강

Syllabus

Reading Mentor Joy Start는 총 3권으로 구성되어 있습니다. 각 권은 총 6개의 Chapter와 18개의 Unit으로 총 8주의 학습 시간으로 구성되어 있습니다. 따라서 Reading Mentor Joy Start는 24주의 학습시간으로 구성되어 있고, 각 권마다 워크북을 제공하여 학습 효율을 높이고자 하였습니다.

Month	Week	Book2	Unit	Contents	Grammar Time
3	4th	Chapter 3 **Nature**	2	Planting a Tree	[look+형용사]의 의미와 쓰임
			3	Flowers in the Garden	반대 의미의 형용사
4	1st	Chapter 4 **Daily Life**	1	Daily Life	일반동사 have의 의미와 쓰임
			2	After School	전치사의 의미와 쓰임
			3	My Dad's Daily Life	관사를 사용하지 않는 명사
	2nd	Chapter 5 **Visiting the Doctor**	1	Animal Clinic	주어가 3인칭 단수일 때 동사의 변화
			2	Toothache	병과 관련된 표현
	3rd		3	Visiting a Doctor	a few/little의 의미와 쓰임
		Chapter 6 **Introducing Yourself**	1	My Name Is Cindy	be동사 과거형과 쓰임
	4th		2	My Name Is Johnson	because와 because of의 의미와 쓰임
			3	My Name Is William	일반동사의 과거형

Month	Week	Book 3	Unit	Contents	Grammar Time
5	1st	Chapter 1 **Clothes**	1	Clothes We Wear	every의 의미와 쓰임
			2	Things to Wear	현재진행형의 부정문
			3	Favorite Clothes	복수형으로 써야 하는 명사
	2nd	Chapter 2 **Sports**	1	Baseball	현재진행형의 의문문
			2	Soccer	be동사의 부정문
	3rd		3	Swimming Pool Rules	일반동사의 부정문과 부정명령문
		Chapter 3 **Seasons and Weather**	1	Seasons	a lot of와 many의 의미와 쓰임
	4th		2	Weather	take와 bring의 의미와 차이
			3	Rainbow	the가 반드시 필요한 단어
6	1st	Chapter 4 **Pets**	1	Her Best Friend	형용사의 어순
			2	Pet Cat	형용사와 부사
			3	Fishbowl	some과 any의 의미와 쓰임
	2nd	Chapter 5 **In the Woods**	1	Trees	[명사+ful] 형태의 형용사
			2	Camping	[like/love+동사ing] 형태
	3rd		3	In the Woods	전치사 from와 to의 의미와 쓰임
		Chapter 6 **Health**	1	Healthy Habits	명사의 복수형
	4th		2	Couch Potato	형용사의 비교급
			3	Good Habits for Our Health	when의 의미와 쓰임

Construction

Reading Mentor Joy Start는 각 권당 6개의 Chapter와 18개 Unit으로 구성되어 있습니다. 각 Unit은 다음과 같이 구성되어 있으며, 부가적으로 워크북을 제공하고 있습니다. 또한 Reading Passage 및 어휘를 녹음한 오디오 파일을 제공하여 생생한 영어 읽기 학습이 되도록 하였습니다.

Reading Passage

각 Chapter마다 3개의 Reading Passage가 있습니다. 수준별 다양한 주제의 이야기들을 읽어보세요. 색감이 풍부한 삽화가 이야기를 더욱 생생하게 느끼게 해줍니다. 또한 음원을 통해서 원어민의 발음으로 직접 들어 보세요.

Reading Check

앞에서 읽은 재미난 이야기를 잘 이해했는지 문제 풀이를 통해서 확인해 보세요.

Word Check

Reading Passage에 등장하는 어휘들을 문제를 통해서 쓰임을 알아보세요. 어휘를 보다 폭넓게 이해할 수 있고 쉽게 암기할 수 있습니다.

Grammar Time

Reading Passage에서 모르고
지나쳤던 문법 사항을 확인해 보
세요. 문장을 확실하게 이해할 수
있습니다.

Review Test

각 Chapter가 끝나면 앞에서 배운 3개의 Reading
Passage와 어휘, 문법 등에 대한 총괄적인 문제를
풀어볼 수 있습니다. 배운 내용을 다시 한 번 복습할
수 있는 기회가 됩니다.

Word Master

다음 Chapter로 넘어가기 전에 잠깐 쉬어 가세요!
어휘는 모든 읽기의 기본입니다. 부담 갖지 마시고
앞에서 배운 단어를 한 번 더 써보고 연습해 보세요.

Answers

정답을 맞춰 보고, 해석과 해설을 통해서
놓친 부분들도 함께 확인해 보세요.

Workbook

별도로 제공되는 워크북은 각 Unit마다 배운 내용을
스스로 풀어보고 연습할 수 있도록 구성했습니다.
스스로 학습할 수 있는 기회로 삼아 보세요.

Contents

Chapter 1

Clothes

TR 3-01

I'm an elementary school student.

When I go to school, I wear my school uniform.

I wear a blue shirt and black pants.

My dad is a businessman.

He wears a suit to work every day.

He also _____ a tie.

My dad looks nice in a suit.

My mom works at a bank.

She wears a uniform every day.

Look! That is my mom.

She looks good in her uniform.

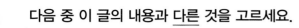
1 다음 중 이 글의 내용과 <u>다른</u> 것을 고르세요.

① 나는 교복을 입고 학교에 간다.

② 나의 교복은 노란 셔츠에 파란색 바지이다.

③ 나의 아버지는 사업을 하신다.

④ 나의 어머니는 은행에서 일을 하신다.

⑤ 나의 어머니는 매일 유니폼을 입는다.

2 다음 중 내 아버지의 모습으로 알맞은 것을 고르세요.

① 　② 　③ 　④ 　⑤

3 다음 중 이 글의 빈칸에 들어갈 알맞은 단어를 고르세요.

① goes　　② buys　　③ sings

④ wears　　⑤ cooks

4 다음 대화의 빈칸에 알맞은 말을 쓰세요.

> **A** Where does your mom work?
>
> **B** My mom works _____.

WORDS

□ **elementary school** 초등학교　□ **wear** 입다　□ **uniform** 유니폼, 제복　□ **shirt** 셔츠

□ **pants** 바지　□ **businessman** 사업가　□ **suit** 정장　□ **every day** 매일

1 다음 중 보기의 단어와 관련 있는 단어를 고르세요.

shirts　　　coats　　　trousers　　　dresses

*trousers 바지

① food　　　　　② clothes　　　　　③ books

④ school　　　　⑤ students

2 다음 단어와 그림을 연결하세요.

(1) 　　(2) 　　(3) 　　(4)

　　•　　　　　　　•　　　　　　　•　　　　　　　•

A. black pants　　　B. tie　　　C. suit　　　D. blue shirt

3 다음 우리말과 같도록 빈칸에 알맞은 단어를 골라 쓰세요.

(1) We _____ uniforms to school. (wear / puts)
　　우리는 교복을 입고 학교에 간다.

(2) My father is a _____. (businessman / doctor)
　　나의 아버지는 사업가다.

(3) My dad looks _____ in a suit. (nice / blue)
　　나의 아빠는 양복을 입은 모습이 멋지다.

GRAMMAR TIME

every의 의미와 쓰임

1 every는 단수명사와 함께 쓰여 '모든', '매', '~마다'라는 의미를 가지고 있습니다.

2 every는 형용사(한정사)로 명사와 함께 사용해야 합니다.

every student 모든 학생

every Sunday 일요일마다

every year 해마다

every morning 매일 아침

3 everyone(모든 사람), everything(모든 것)은 대명사로 단독으로 쓰일 수 있습니다.

Everyone in her class likes K-pop music.

그녀 반의 모든 사람은 케이팝 음악을 좋아한다.

---

1 다음 중 우리말과 같도록 빈칸에 들어갈 알맞은 말을 고르세요.

> _____ in the room likes you.
>
> 방에 있는 모든 사람이 너를 좋아한다.

① People   ② Everyone   ③ Every student

④ Everything   ⑤ They

---

2 다음 우리말과 같도록 괄호 안에서 알맞은 것을 고르세요.

(1) There are people from every (country / countries) here.

각국에서 온 사람들이 여기 있다.

(2) She knows (every / everyone) student in the classroom.

그녀는 교실의 모든 학생을 안다.

(3) I go to the beach every (Sunday / Sundays).

나는 매주 일요일 해변에 간다.

TR 3-02

Jessica is wearing a swimming suit and a swimming cap.

She is swimming in the pool.

She can swim very fast.

Jessie is wearing a helmet.

She is riding a bike.

She enjoys riding a bike.

Mr. Donovan is wearing a seatbelt.

He is driving a car.

He drives carefully.

My grandmother is wearing glasses.

She is reading a book.

She likes reading books.

READING CHECK

1 다음 문장이 이 글의 내용과 같으면 T에 동그라미를, 다르면 F에 동그라미 하세요.

(1) Jessica is a fast swimmer.　　　　T　　F

(2) Mr. Donovan is a careful driver.　　T　　F

(3) Jessie is buying a bike.　　　　　 T　　F

2 다음 중 그림에서 Jessie를 고르세요.

① 　② 　③ 　④　⑤

3 다음 중 보기의 두 문장이 의미가 같도록 빈칸에 들어갈 알맞은 말을 고르세요.

My grandmother likes reading books.
= My grandmother's _____ is reading books.

① car　　　　② hobby　　　③ hair　　　④ room　　　⑤ cat

4 다음 대화의 빈칸에 알맞은 말을 쓰세요.

A What is Mr. Donovan doing?
B He's _____.

WORDS

□ **wear** 입다, 쓰다　□ **swimming suit** 수영복　□ **swimming cap** 수영모자　□ **pool** 수영장

□ **helmet** 헬멧　□ **ride** 타다　□ **enjoy** 즐기다　□ **seatbelt** 안전벨트　□ **carefully** 조심스럽게

□ **glasses** 안경

1 다음 단어와 그림을 연결하세요.

(1)  (2)  (3)   (4)

•   •   •   •

•   •   •   •

A. swimming cap   B. ride a bike   C. glasses   D. drive a car

2 다음 중 우리말과 같도록 빈칸에 들어갈 알맞은 말을 고르세요.

> He drives _____. 그는 조심스럽게 운전한다.

① really   ② fast   ③ slowly
④ easily   ⑤ carefully

3 다음 중 우리말과 같도록 빈칸에 알맞은 단어를 골라 쓰세요.

(1) Jessie is wearing a _____. (helmet / hat)
제시는 헬멧을 쓰고 있다.

(2) She _____ riding a bike. (interests / enjoys)
그녀는 자전거 타는 것을 즐긴다.

(3) He is wearing a _____. (seatbelt / leather belt)
그는 안전벨트를 착용하고 있다.

GRAMMAR TIME

현재진행형의 부정문

1. 현재 일어나고 있는 동작을 설명할 때 현재진행형을 씁니다.

2. 현재진행형의 부정문은 [주어+be동사+not+-ing]의 형태로 씁니다.

3. be동사는 주어에 따라 맞춰 씁니다.

I	am not	
You	are not (aren't)	dancing.
He / She / It	is not (isn't)	춤을 추고 있지 않다.
We / They	are not (aren't)	

4. 진행형은 대부분의 동사 뒤에 ing를 붙이나 e로 끝나는 동사는 e를 지우고 ing를 씁니다.
   예) dance → dancing

1

다음 중 빈칸에 들어갈 알맞은 말을 고르세요.

The children are not _____ baseball.

① play   ② plays   ③ playing
④ is playing   ⑤ are playing

2

다음 우리말과 같도록 밑줄 친 부분을 바르게 고치세요.

(1) Sam isn't <u>talk</u> to his friends.   → _____
   샘은 친구들과 얘기를 하고 있지 않다.

(2) Helen <u>aren't</u> crying in her room.   → _____
   헬렌이 그녀의 방에서 울고 있지 않다.

(3) The children are not <u>play</u> outside.   → _____
   그 아이들이 바깥에서 놀고 있지 않다.

(4) The boys aren't <u>sing</u> on stage now.   → _____
   그 소년들이 지금 무대 위에서 노래하고 있지 않다.

TR 3-03

Karl likes his school uniform.

It is very comfortable and cool.

The school uniform is a blue shirt with black shorts or a skirt.

There is a school logo on the shirt.

He also likes blue jeans.

He wears blue jeans when he goes out.

He doesn't need a coat and a sweater in winter.

He lives in Indonesia.

It is very hot all year round in Indonesia.

He hopes to wear a coat someday.

READING CHECK

1 다음 문장이 이 글의 내용과 같으면 T에 동그라미를, 다르면 F에 동그라미 하세요.

(1) Karl wears a uniform to school.　　　　T　　F

(2) Karl likes to wear a coat when he goes out.　　T　　F

(3) Indonesia's weather is hot all year round.　　T　　F

2 다음 중 Karl이 코트가 필요하지 <u>않은</u> 이유를 고르세요.

① He has a lot of coats.
② He lives in a hot climate.
③ He doesn't like to wear a coat.
④ He is too young to wear a coat.
⑤ He is going to move to Indonesia.

3 다음 중 Karl의 학교 교복으로 알맞은 그림을 고르세요.

① ② ③ ④ ⑤

4 다음 대화의 빈칸에 알맞은 말을 쓰세요.

A What does Karl wear when he goes out?
B He wears _____.

WORDS

□ **comfortable** 편안한　□ **cool** 멋진　□ **shorts** 반바지　□ **skirt** 치마　□ **logo** 로고

□ **blue jeans** 청바지　□ **go out** 외출하다　□ **coat** 코트　□ **sweater** 스웨터　□ **someday** 언젠가

1 다음 단어와 그림을 연결하세요.

(1)  (2)  (3)  (4)

- • • • •

A. skirt   B. blues jeans   C. sweater   D. hot

2 다음 중 보기의 빈칸에 들어갈 알맞은 단어를 고르세요.

> Tom likes to sleep on the sofa.
> The sofa is very soft.
> He feels _____ when he sleeps on the sofa.

① comfortable   ② careful   ③ bad
④ sad   ⑤ hungry

3 다음 우리말과 같도록 빈칸에 알맞은 단어를 골라 쓰세요.

(1) There is a school _____ on the shirt. (logo / button)
그 셔츠에 학교 로고가 있다.

(2) He wears blue jeans when he _____. (comes in / goes out)
그는 외출할 때 청바지를 입는다.

(3) It is very hot _____ round in Indonesia. (all year / month)
인도네시아는 1년 내내 매우 덥다.

GRAMMAR TIME

복수형으로 써야 하는 명사

1 짝을 이루고 있거나 두 부분이 하나를 이루고 있는 옷이나 도구들은 복수형으로 써야 합니다.

glasses 안경	socks 양말	shoes 신발
blue jeans 청바지	scissors 가위	pants 바지
shorts 반바지	gloves 장갑	stockings 스타킹

2 복수형 명사의 수를 셀 때는 a pair of ~, two pairs of ~의 형태로 나타냅니다.
a pair of shoes 신발 한 켤레
a pair of blue jeans 청바지 하나
two pairs of socks 양말 두 켤레

---

1 다음 중 우리말과 같도록 빈칸에 들어갈 알맞은 말을 고르세요.

> I need _____ of socks. 나는 양말 3켤레가 필요하다.

① three   ② a pair   ③ pairs
④ three pair   ⑤ three pairs

2 다음 우리말과 같도록 밑줄 친 부분을 바르게 고치세요.

(1) Sam is wearing glass.   → _____
    샘은 안경을 쓰고 있다.

(2) I want to buy these yellow glove.   → _____
    나는 이 노란 장갑들을 사고 싶다.

(3) We need two pair of shoes.   → _____
    우리는 신발 두 켤레가 필요하다.

[01-02] 다음 중 빈칸에 들어갈 알맞은 말을 고르세요.

01

They are not _____ TV now.

① watch   ② watches   ③ watching

④ watched   ⑤ is watching

02

I need a _____ of shoes.

① two   ② some   ③ a pairs

④ pairs   ⑤ pair

03 다음 중 빈칸에 올 수 <u>없는</u> 말을 고르세요.

I'm going to buy two pairs of _____.

① pants   ② bread   ③ scissors

④ shoes   ⑤ socks

04 다음 중 밑줄 친 것이 올바르지 <u>않은</u> 것을 고르세요.

① Sam is wearing <u>glasses</u>.

② Sam isn't <u>talking</u> to his teacher.

③ She knows <u>every</u> student in the classroom.

④ <u>Everyone</u> in the room is playing computer games.

⑤ I go to the beach every <u>Sundays</u>.

[05-06] 다음 중 우리말과 같도록 빈칸에 들어갈 알맞은 말을 고르세요.

05

> It's such a _____ bed. 이것은 정말 편안한 침대다.

① expensive 　　② comfortable 　　③ diligent
④ careful 　　⑤ important

06

> You look _____ in the dress. 너는 그 옷이 잘 어울린다.

① careful 　　② nice 　　③ fun
④ full 　　⑤ bad

07 다음 중 빈칸에 들어갈 알맞은 말을 고르세요.

> Donovan is in the car.
> He is wearing a _____.

① pants 　　② glasses 　　③ seatbelt
④ gloves 　　⑤ scissors

08 다음 중 그림을 보고 빈칸에 들어갈 알맞은 말을 고르세요.

> It is very _____ today.

① rainy 　　② windy 　　③ cool
④ hot 　　⑤ cold

Karl likes his school uniform.

It is very comfortable and cool.

The school uniform is a blue shirt with black shorts or a skirt.

There is a school logo on the shirt.

He also likes blue jeans.

He wears blue jeans when he goes out.

He doesn't need a coat and a sweater in winter, _____ he lives in a tropical area.

*tropical 열대의

09 다음 중 이 글에서 언급하지 <u>않은</u> 것을 고르세요.

① Karl의 교복 색깔　　　　　② Karl이 좋아하는 옷의 종류

③ 외투가 필요하지 않은 이유　　④ Karl이 사는 지역

⑤ Karl의 학교 이름

10 다음 중 이 글의 빈칸에 들어갈 알맞은 말을 고르세요.

① but　　　　　② and　　　　　③ so

④ when　　　　⑤ because

11 다음 중 빈칸에 공통으로 들어갈 알맞은 말을 고르세요.

> ・ My mom looks good _____ her uniform.
> ・ She is swimming _____ the pool.

① at　　　　　② in　　　　　③ of

④ on　　　　　⑤ to

12 다음 보기에서 빈칸에 들어갈 알맞을 말을 골라 쓰세요.

ride	coat	need

(1) Can you _____ a bike?

(2) We _____ some money.

(3) She bought me a new _____.

13 다음 보기의 밑줄 친 부분을 바르게 고치세요.

I want to buy a pair of glove.

_____

14 다음 우리말과 같도록 빈칸에 알맞은 말을 쓰세요.

Jim _____ reading a book now. 짐은 지금 책을 읽고 있지 않다.

_____

15 다음 영어를 우리말로 쓰세요.

(1) He hopes to wear a coat someday.

_____

(2) He wears a suit to work every day.

_____

📍 다음 단어의 뜻을 쓰고, 단어를 세 번씩 더 써보세요.

01 businessman	사업가	businessman	businessman	businessman
02 carefully				
03 comfortable				
04 cool				
05 enjoy				
06 helmet				
07 pants				
08 pool				
09 seatbelt				
10 shorts				
11 skirt				
12 someday				
13 suit				
14 sweater				
15 uniform				

Chapter 2

Sports

Ted is playing baseball with his friends.

He's a pitcher.

He's throwing a ball to the catcher.

James is a batter.

He has a bat.

He is wearing a helmet.

He tries to hit the ball with the bat.

Tom is an outfielder.

He has a baseball glove.

His job is to catch the ball with his glove.

James hits the ball and the ball is flying to Tom.

Oh, he misses the ball.

TR 3-04

READING CHECK

1 다음 문장이 이 글의 내용과 같으면 T에 동그라미를, 다르면 F에 동그라미 하세요.

(1) Ted is throwing a ball to Tom. T F

(2) James has a bat and he tries to hit the ball with it. T F

(3) Tom's job is to catch the ball with his glove. T F

2 다음 중 밑줄 친 **misses**의 반대말을 고르세요. (동사원형)

① hit ② live ③ throw

④ catch ⑤ wear

3 다음 중 Ted의 포지션으로 알맞은 그림을 고르세요.

①  ②  ③   ④   ⑤

4 다음 대화의 빈칸에 Yes나 No로 대답하세요.

A Did Tom catch the ball with his glove?

B _____ .

WORDS

□ **baseball** 야구 □ **pitcher** 투수 □ **throw** 던지다 □ **catcher** 포수 □ **batter** 타자

□ **bat** 야구방망이 □ **outfielder** 외야수 □ **glove** 글러브 □ **catch** 잡다 □ **miss** 놓치다

WORD CHECK

1 다음 단어와 그림을 연결하세요.

(1)  (2)  (3)  (4)

A. throw a ball B. a baseball glove C. catch a ball D. hit a ball

2 다음 중 우리말과 같도록 빈칸에 들어갈 알맞은 말을 고르세요.

> Tony is _____ a cap. 토니는 모자를 쓰고 있다.

① buying   ② wearing   ③ catching
④ throwing   ⑤ hitting

3 다음 우리말과 같도록 빈칸에 알맞은 단어를 골라 쓰세요.

(1) He's throwing a ball to the _____. (pitcher / catcher)
그는 포수에게 공을 던지고 있다.

(2) He _____ to hit the ball with the bat. (tries / has)
그는 방망이로 공을 치려고 한다.

(3) James hits the ball and the ball is _____ to Tom.
제임스가 볼을 치고, 그 볼은 톰에게 날아가고 있다.   (flying / throwing)

GRAMMAR TIME

현재진행형의 의문문

1 현재 일어나고 있는 동작에 대해 물을 때 현재진행형 의문문을 씁니다.

2 '~하고 있나요?', '~하는 중인가요?'라는 의미입니다.

3 be동사를 주어 앞에 보내고, 주어 다음에 진행형을 쓰고 물음표를 붙입니다.

Am	+ 주어	+ dancing?
Are	(I / we / you / they	춤을 추고 있니?
Is	he / she / it)	

Ted is playing baseball. 테드는 야구를 하고 있다.

→ **Is** Ted **playing** baseball? 테드는 야구를 하고 있니?

He is wearing a helmet. 그는 헬멧을 쓰고 있다.

→ **Is** he **wearing** a helmet? 그는 헬멧을 쓰고 있니?

---

1 다음 현재진행형을 의문문으로 만들 때, 빈칸에 알맞은 말을 쓰세요.

(1) You are reading a book.

→ ＿＿＿＿＿＿＿＿＿＿＿＿＿＿＿＿＿ reading a book?

(2) He is swimming.

→ ＿＿＿＿＿＿＿＿＿＿＿＿＿＿＿＿＿ swimming?

(3) They are crying.

→ Are ＿＿＿＿＿＿＿＿＿＿＿＿＿＿＿ ?

(4) Sam is playing table tennis.

→ ＿＿＿＿＿＿＿＿＿＿＿＿＿＿＿＿＿ table tennis?

(5) She is cooking.

→ Is ＿＿＿＿＿＿＿＿＿＿＿＿＿＿＿ ?

TR 3-05

Soccer is Mina's favorite sport.

She's playing soccer with her friends.

They're wearing uniforms and soccer shoes.

Mina passes the ball to Karl.

Karl dribbles the ball to the goal and shoots.

Steve grabs the ball with his hands.

He can use his hands.

He is the goalkeeper.

Donovan blows the whistle.

He is the referee.

Cathy and I are sitting in the stands.

We are not good at soccer.

But we like watching soccer games.

1 다음 문장이 이 글의 내용과 같으면 T에 동그라미를, 다르면 F에 동그라미 하세요.

(1) Mina and her friends are on the soccer field.   T   F

(2) Donovan is on the soccer field but he isn't a player.   T   F

(3) Cathy is a good soccer player.   T   F

2 다음 중 빈칸에 들어갈 알맞은 말을 고르세요.

> Cathy and I are sitting in the stands _____.

① to watch a soccer game   ② to take a picture
③ to play soccer   ④ to blow a whistle
⑤ to listen to music

3 다음 중 Steve의 모습으로 알맞은 그림을 고르세요.

①   ②    ③   ④    ⑤

4 다음 대화의 빈칸에 알맞은 말을 쓰세요.

> A What is Mina's favorite sport?
> B Her favorite sport is _____.

WORDS
□ **soccer** 축구   □ **pass** 패스하다   □ **dribble** 드리블하다   □ **shoot** 슛하다   □ **grab** 잡다   □ **use** 사용하다
□ **goalkeeper** 골키퍼   □ **whistle** 호루라기   □ **referee** 심판   □ **stand** 관람석

WORD CHECK

1 다음 단어와 그림을 연결하세요.

(1)    (2)    (3)    (4)

•   •   •   •

A. soccer shoes   B. shoot   C. grab a ball   D. sitting in the stands

2 다음 중 우리말과 같도록 빈칸에 들어갈 알맞은 단어를 고르세요.

> I am not _____ at math. 나는 수학을 잘하지 못한다.

① fast   ② enough   ③ too
④ bad   ⑤ good

3 다음 우리말과 같도록 빈칸에 알맞은 단어를 골라 쓰세요.

(1) Steve _____ the ball with his hands. (grabs / hits)
스티브는 손으로 공을 잡는다.

(2) Donovan _____ the whistle. (dribbles / blows)
도노반은 호루라기를 분다.

(3) We like _____ soccer games. (reading / watching)
우리는 축구 경기 보는 것을 좋아한다.

GRAMMAR TIME

be동사의 부정문

1 be동사 다음에는 명사나 형용사가 옵니다.

2 주어가 '~이 아니다'라고 표현할 때 not을 be동사 다음에 씁니다.

	현재	과거
I	am not = 'm not	was not = wasn't
He / She / It / 단수명사	is not = isn't	was not = wasn't
We / You / They / 복수명사	are not = aren't	were not = weren't

She **is** a doctor. 그녀는 의사다. (긍정문)

She **is not** a doctor. 그녀는 의사가 아니다. (부정문)

3 be동사와 not을 줄여서 사용할 수 있습니다.

She **isn't** a doctor. 그녀는 의사가 아니다.

The boys **aren't** hungry. 그 소년들은 배고프지 않다.

---

1 다음 중 우리말과 같도록 빈칸에 들어갈 알맞은 말을 고르세요.

> We _____ doctors. We are nurses.
>
> 우리는 의사들이 아니다. 우리는 간호사들이다.

① is not   ② am not   ③ isn't

④ aren't   ⑤ it's not

2 다음 문장을 부정문으로 바꾸세요.

(1) My dad is tall.

➡ _____

(2) They are ready for school.

➡ _____

(3) We were in the parking lot.

➡ _____

Safety Rules in the Swimming Pool

TR 3-06

1 Wear a swimsuit and a swimming cap.

2 Always follow the lifeguard's directions.

3 Don't run in the pool area.

4 Don't bring animals into the pool area.

5 Don't eat in the pool area.

6 Take a shower before entering the swimming pool.

7 Do warm-ups before entering the swimming pool.

8 Use the pool ladder to enter and exit the swimming pool.

9 Don't dive into the swimming pool.

POOL RULES

NO PETS	NO DIVING	DON'T SWIM ALONE	NO LITTERING	DON'T RUN
NO SMOKING	NO FOOD	NO DRINK	NO PEEING IN POOL	NO ROUGH PLAY
8.30 AM 22.00 PM	USE RESTROOMS	USE SLIPPERS	USE CAP AND GOGGLES	BE CAREFULL
USE THE STAIRS	SHOWER BEFORE POOL	CHILDREN ONLY WITH PARENTS	USE SWIMSUIT	WATCH YOUR CHILDREN

1 다음 중 이 글이 무엇에 관한 내용인지 고르세요.

① safety rules in the science lab ② rules in the classroom
③ rules in the school library ④ safety rules in the swimming pool
⑤ how to swim in the sea

2 다음 중 수영 전에 해야 할 일로 알맞은 것을 고르세요.

① running in the pool area ② eating snacks in the pool area
③ diving ④ listening to music
⑤ warming-up

3 다음 중 이 글에서 수영장에서 지켜야 할 규칙으로 언급하지 <u>않은</u> 것을 고르세요.

①
NO DIVING

②
SHOWER BEFORE POOL

③
NO SMOKING

④
USE THE STAIRS

⑤
DON'T RUN

4 다음 대화의 빈칸에 알맞은 말을 쓰세요.

A What do you have to use when you exit a pool?
B We have to _____.

WORDS

□ **safety rule** 안전 규칙 □ **lifeguard** 안전요원 □ **direction** 지시 □ **pool** 수영장 □ **area** 구역, 지역

□ **enter** 들어가다 □ **warm-up** 준비운동 □ **ladder** 사다리 □ **exit** 나가다 □ **dive** 다이빙하다

1 다음 단어와 그림을 연결하세요.

(1) 　　(2) 　　(3) 　　(4)

A. lifeguard　　B. warm-up　　C. dive　　D. ladder

2 다음 중 보기가 설명하고 있는 것을 고르세요.

> There is a large hole in the ground.
> The hole is filled with water.
> People can swim in it.

① river　　　　② sea　　　　　③ swimming pool
④ gym　　　　⑤ playground

3 다음 우리말과 같도록 빈칸에 알맞은 단어를 골라 쓰세요.

(1) Always follow the lifeguard's _____. (talks / directions)
항상 안전요원의 지시를 따르라.

(2) Take a shower before _____ the swimming pool.
수영장에 들어가기 전에 샤워를 해라.　　　　　　(entering / going)

(3) Don't _____ animals into the pool area. (bring / exit)
수영장 근처에 동물을 데리고 오지 마라.

GRAMMAR TIME

일반동사의 부정문과 부정명령문

1 일반동사가 쓰인 현재시제의 문장을 부정문으로 만들기 위해서는 일반동사 앞에 don't 또는 doesn't를 씁니다.

2 don't과 doesn't 뒤에는 반드시 동사원형이 와야 합니다.

I / You	don't	eat fast food. 패스트푸드를 먹지 않는다.
He / She / It	doesn't	
We / They	don't	

3 부정명령문은 상대방(You)에게 '~을 하지 마라'라는 의미를 전달하는 형태이므로 You를 생략하고 Don't가 문장 앞에 옵니다.

Don't eat fast food. 패스트푸드를 먹지 마라.

Don't talk in class. 수업 중에 떠들지 마라.

1 다음 괄호 안에서 알맞은 것을 고르세요.

(1) They (don't / doesn't) eat vegetables.

(2) My mother (don't / doesn't) listen to the radio.

(3) I (don't / doesn't) like going shopping.

(4) (Don't / Doesn't) drink this soda.

(5) Don't (be / is) late for school again.

2 다음 문장을 부정문으로 바꾸세요.

> The cake tastes good.

[01-03] 다음 중 우리말과 같도록 빈칸에 들어갈 알맞은 말을 고르세요.

01
They _____ my friends. They are my cousins.
그들은 나의 친구들이 아니다. 그들은 나의 사촌들이다.

① is not ② am not ③ isn't
④ aren't ⑤ don't

02
My mother _____ watch TV.
나의 엄마는 TV를 보지 않는다.

① isn't ② am not ③ aren't
④ don't ⑤ doesn't

03
She _____ at the party yesterday.
그녀는 어제 파티에 없었다.

① is not ② aren't ③ wasn't
④ weren't ⑤ isn't

04 다음 중 밑줄 친 것이 올바르지 <u>않은</u> 것을 고르세요.
① <u>Is</u> Sam playing table tennis?
② <u>Are</u> they reading books now?
③ Don't <u>talks</u> in class.
④ We <u>don't</u> eat vegetables.
⑤ They <u>are not</u> my parents.

[05-06] 다음 중 우리말과 같도록 빈칸에 들어갈 알맞은 말을 고르세요.

05

Always _____ the lifeguard's directions.

항상 안전요원의 지시를 따라라.

① use   ② enter   ③ follow
④ bring   ⑤ feed

06

His job is to _____ the ball with his glove.

그의 일은 글러브로 공을 잡는 것이다.

① hit   ② catch   ③ use
④ fly   ⑤ give

07 다음 중 빈칸에 들어갈 알맞은 말을 고르세요.

Steve is a goalkeeper. He can grab the ball with his _____.

① back   ② legs   ③ hands
④ glove   ⑤ head

08 다음 중 그림을 보고 빈칸에 들어갈 알맞은 말을 고르세요.

Mike _____ the whistle.

① blows   ② sings   ③ takes
④ throws   ⑤ wears

[09-10] **다음을 읽고 질문에 답하세요.**

> Safety Rules in the Swimming Pool
> 1 Don't run in the pool area.
> 2 Don't eat in the pool area.
> 3 <u>Don't bring animals into the pool area.</u>
> 4 Don't dive into the swimming pool.
> 5 Don't swallow pool water.
> 6 Don't swim alone.
>
>
> NO DIVING

09 **다음 중 이 글에서 언급하지 <u>않은</u> 것을 고르세요.**

① 수영장에서 뛰지 마라. ② 수영장에서 음식 먹지 마라.

③ 다이빙하지 마라. ④ 수영장 물을 삼키지 마라.

⑤ 수영장에서 소리 지르지 마라.

10 **다음 중 이 글의 밑줄 친 문장과 의미가 같은 것을 고르세요.**

① Don't feed animals. ② Don't eat meat.

③ No kids zone. ④ No smoking zone.

⑤ No pets allowed.

11 **다음 중 빈칸에 공통으로 들어갈 알맞은 말을 고르세요.**

> · Take a shower _____ entering the swimming pool.
> · Do warm-ups _____ entering the swimming pool.

① in ② before ③ because of

④ after ⑤ while

12 다음 보기에서 빈칸에 들어갈 알맞을 말을 골라 쓰세요.

enter	fly	throw

(1) Don't _____ stones at the birds.

(2) Can I _____ the room?

(3) I want to _____ in the sky like birds.

13 다음 밑줄 친 부분을 바르게 고치세요.

Sam and I <u>am not</u> good at soccer.

_____

14 다음 우리말과 같도록 주어진 단어를 이용하여 문장을 완성하세요.

_____ the red button. (touch) 빨간색 단추를 건드리지 마라.

_____

15 다음 영어를 우리말로 쓰세요.

(1) Mina passes the ball to Karl.

_____

(2) He hits the ball with the bat.

_____

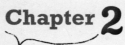

TR 3-06-W

다음 단어의 뜻을 쓰고, 단어를 세 번씩 더 써보세요.

01	area	구역, 지역	area	area	area
02	baseball				
03	catcher				
04	enter				
05	exit				
06	glove				
07	grab				
08	ladder				
09	lifeguard				
10	outfielder				
11	pitcher				
12	referee				
13	soccer				
14	throw				
15	whistle				

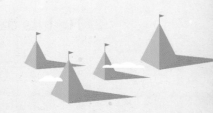

Chapter 3

Seasons and Weather

TR 3-07

There are four seasons in a year.

They are spring, summer, fall, and winter.

Spring is warm.

We can see a lot of flowers in spring.

Summer is hot.

We can swim in the sea.

Fall is cool.

We can see the colorful leaves in the mountains.

Winter is cold.

We can make a snowman in winter.

What's your favorite season?

1 다음 중 이 글이 무엇에 관한 내용인지 고르세요.

① flowers in spring　　　　② my favorite sport

③ colorful leaves　　　　④ my favorite season

⑤ four seasons

2 다음 중 밑줄 친 **a lot of**와 의미가 같은 단어를 고르세요.

① very　　　　② many　　　　③ beautiful

④ old　　　　⑤ warm

3 이 글에서 hot과 반대되는 의미의 말을 찾아 쓰세요.

_____

4 다음 대화의 빈칸에 알맞은 말을 쓰세요.

> **A** How many seasons are there in a year?
>
> **B** There are _____.

WORDS

☐ **season** 계절　☐ **year** 1년　☐ **spring** 봄　☐ **summer** 여름　☐ **fall** 가을　☐ **winter** 겨울

☐ **warm** 따뜻한　☐ **sea** 바다　☐ **cool** 시원한　☐ **colorful** 형형색색의　☐ **leaf** 나뭇잎(복수형 leaves)

☐ **mountain** 산　☐ **snowman** 눈사람

1 다음 단어와 그림을 연결하세요.

(1)  (2)  (3)  (4)

·   ·   ·   ·

·   ·   ·   ·

A. summer   B. colorful leaves   C. snowman   D. winter

2 다음 보기가 설명하고 있는 계절을 쓰세요.

This is the season between spring and fall.

The weather is usually hot.

We go to the beach to swim.

_____

3 다음 우리말과 같도록 빈칸에 알맞은 단어를 골라 쓰세요.

(1) There are four _____ in a year. (seasons / reasons)
1년에는 4계절이 있다.

(2) We can see a lot of flowers in _____ . (fall / spring)
우리는 봄에 많은 꽃들을 볼 수 있다.

(3) We can see the colorful _____ in the mountains.
우리는 산에서 형형색색의 나뭇잎들을 볼 수 있다.   (leaves / clothes)

a lot of와 many의 의미와 쓰임

1 a lot of와 many는 모두 '많은'이란 의미를 가지고 있지만 쓰임이 조금 다릅니다.

2 a lot of 다음에는 복수명사와 셀 수 없는 명사가 올 수 있습니다.

3 many 다음에는 복수명사만 올 수 있습니다.

a lot of+복수명사 / 셀 수 없는 명사	**a lot of** cars 많은 자동차들 **a lot of** water 많은 물
many+복수명사	**many** cars 많은 자동차들 **many** students 많은 학생들

4 셀 수 없는 명사 – 셀 수 없는 명사는 복수형을 만들 수 없습니다.
water, money, salt, meat, milk, juice, cheese 등이 셀 수 없는 명사입니다.

1 다음 괄호 안에서 알맞은 것을 고르세요.

(1) There are many (student / students) in the gym.

(2) I have (a lot of / many) money.

(3) There is (a lot of / many) water in the tank.

(4) There is (a lot of / many) salt in the jar.

2 다음 중 빈칸에 올 수 <u>없는</u> 것을 고르세요.

I don't have many _____.

① books　　　　② friends　　　　③ money
④ bags　　　　⑤ pencils

TR 3-08

It's <u>sunny</u> today.

There are no clouds in the sky.

I love sunny weather.

It's rainy today.

The rain is falling from the sky.

I need an umbrella today.

It's snowy today.

The ground is covered with _____.

I love making a snowman with my friends.

It's cloudy.

There are a lot of dark clouds in the sky.

It's going to rain this afternoon.

Don't forget to take your umbrella when you go out.

1 다음 문장이 이 글의 내용과 같으면 T에 동그라미를, 다르면 F에 동그라미 하세요.

(1) When it's sunny, we don't need an umbrella.　　　T　　F

(2) When it rains, the rain falls from the sky.　　　T　　F

(3) We can make a snowman in summer.　　　T　　F

2 다음 중 이 글의 빈칸에 들어갈 알맞은 단어를 고르세요.

① rain　　　② snow　　　③ clouds
④ leaves　　　⑤ sunlight

3 다음 중 밑줄 친 sunny와 의미가 유사한 단어를 고르세요.

① rainy　　　② snowy　　　③ clear
④ funny　　　⑤ dark

4 다음 대화의 빈칸에 알맞은 말을 쓰세요.

> A What's the weather like today?
> B It's ＿＿＿＿＿＿＿. There are dark clouds in the sky.

WORDS

□ **sunny** 맑은　□ **cloud** 구름　□ **sky** 하늘　□ **weather** 날씨　□ **fall** 떨어지다　□ **umbrella** 우산

□ **snowy** 눈이 오는　□ **cover** 덮다　□ **snowman** 눈사람　□ **cloudy** 흐린　□ **dark** 어두운

□ **forget** 잊다　□ **go out** 외출하다

1 다음 보기의 단어를 이용하여 그림과 알맞은 단어를 쓰세요.

> sunny   cloudy   rainy   snowy

(1) _____

(2) _____

(3) _____

(4) _____

2 다음 중 빈칸에 들어갈 알맞은 단어를 고르세요.

> Stars are twinkling in the _____.

① rain   ② sky   ③ cloud

④ snow   ⑤ road

3 다음 우리말과 같도록 빈칸에 알맞은 단어를 골라 쓰세요.

(1) There are _____ clouds in the sky. (no / some)
하늘에 구름 한 점 없다.

(2) The rain is _____ from the sky. (falling / flying)
비가 하늘에서 떨어진다.

(3) There are a lot of _____ clouds in the sky. (dark / white)
하늘에 많은 먹구름이 있다.

GRAMMAR TIME

take와 bring의 의미와 차이

1 take는 관점의 중심이 되는 사람에게서 멀어지는 것을 의미하고 bring은 관점의 중심이 되는 사람에게 가까워지는 것을 의미합니다.

2 take는 '(어떤 것을 한 곳에서 다른 곳으로) 가져가다', '데려가다'라는 의미이고, bring은 '가져오다', '데려오다'라는 의미입니다.

·Can you **take** this and put it away?
이거 가져가서 치워줄 수 있나요?

Can you **bring** the book to me?
그 책을 내게 가져올 수 있나요?

1 다음 우리말과 같도록 빈칸에 take나 bring을 쓰세요.

(1) They _____ me to the hospital.
그들은 나를 병원에 데려간다.

(2) _____ the book with you.
그 책을 가져가라.

(3) Please _____ your son to the party.
파티에 아들을 데려오세요.

(4) Can you _____ me the cookies?
저 쿠키들을 내게 가져올래?

(5) Don't forget to _____ your homework tomorrow.
내일 숙제 가지고 오는 거 까먹지 마.

(6) Can you _____ me to the airport?
공항까지 데려가 줄 수 있나요?

UNIT 3 Rainbow

TR 3-09

Look over there!

There is a rainbow in the sky.

We can sometimes see a rainbow in the sky when it's raining.

A rainbow is an arch of seven different colors.

<u>They</u> are red, orange, yellow, green, blue, indigo, and violet.

The _____ of the rainbow look very beautiful.

A rainbow is actually round like a circle,

but we can only see half of the rainbow.

I like rainbows.

A rainbow is a symbol of hope and happiness.

Today is a lucky day.

1 다음 문장이 이 글의 내용과 같으면 T에 동그라미를, 다르면 F에 동그라미 하세요.

(1) We can see a rainbow when it's raining.　　　T　　F

(2) I feel sad when I see a rainbow.　　　T　　F

(3) A rainbow is made of seven colors.　　　T　　F

2 다음 중 밑줄 친 **They**가 의미하는 것을 고르세요.

① rainbows　　　　　　② seven different colors

③ an arch　　　　　　④ sunlight

⑤ sky

3 다음 중 이 글의 빈칸에 들어갈 알맞은 단어를 고르세요.

① colors　　　② circles　　　③ rains

④ curves　　　⑤ luck

4 다음 대화의 빈칸에 알맞은 말을 쓰세요.

> **A** How many colors are there in a rainbow?
> **B** There _____ in a rainbow.

WORDS

□ **rainbow** 무지개　□ **sometimes** 때때로　□ **arch** 아치　□ **different** 다른　□ **color** 색깔

□ **indigo** 남색　□ **violet** 보라색　□ **actually** 실제로　□ **half** 반, 절반　□ **symbol** 상징

□ **hope** 희망　□ **happiness** 행복　□ **lucky** 운이 좋은

1 다음 단어와 그림을 연결하세요.

(1)

(2)

(3)

(4)

A. rainbow   B. blue   C. colors   D. arch

2 다음 보기가 나타내는 단어를 쓰세요.

arch	rain	seven colors	sky

_____

3 다음 우리말과 같도록 빈칸에 알맞은 단어를 골라 쓰세요.

(1) A rainbow is actually _____ like a circle.

실제로 무지개는 원처럼 둥근 모양이다.   (round / square)

(2) A rainbow is an arch of seven _____ colors.

무지개는 7개의 다른 색이 있는 아치다.   (different / same)

(3) A rainbow is a _____ of hope and happiness.

무지개는 희망과 행복의 상징이다.   (gift / symbol)

the가 반드시 필요한 단어

1 정관사 the는 '그 ~'라는 의미로 명사 앞에 쓸 수 있습니다.

2 그 중에서 정관사 the를 반드시 써야 하는 명사들이 있습니다.

세상에 하나밖에 없는 것	the sun	the moon	the world	the sky 등
play, practice 앞에 오는 악기 이름 앞에	the piano	the violin	the guitar	the cello 등
위치, 방향 앞에	the left the south	the right the north 등	the east	the west
아침, 오후, 저녁을 표현할 때	in **the** morning	in **the** afternoon	in **the** evening 등	

Look at **the** sky. 하늘을 봐라.

I play **the** piano every day. 나는 매일 피아노를 연주한다.

The sun sets in **the** west. 태양은 서쪽으로 진다.

The store closes in **the** evening. 그 상점은 저녁에 닫는다.

---

1 다음 보기에서 반드시 the를 붙여야 하는 단어를 골라 쓰세요.

ring	moon	China	baseball	stamps
cook	rice	flowers	sun	world
sky	actor	day	Sunday	family
north	truck	east	flour	west

---

2 다음 밑줄 친 부분을 바르게 고치세요.

(1) <u>A moon</u> is very bright.   → _____

달은 무척 밝다.

(2) She <u>plays a guitar</u> after school.   → _____

그녀는 방과 후에 기타를 친다.

(3) We get up early <u>in a morning</u>.   → _____

우리는 아침 일찍 일어난다.

Review Test

Answers p.9

01 다음 중 빈칸에 알맞지 <u>않은</u> 것을 고르세요.

> There are many _____ in the school.

① desks   ② students   ③ trees
④ classrooms   ⑤ teacher

[02-03] 다음 중 빈칸에 들어갈 알맞은 말을 고르세요.

02
> Tony plays _____ piano after school.

① a   ② an   ③ the
④ in   ⑤ at

03
> She has _____ money.

① so   ② many   ③ a lot of
④ very   ⑤ a lot

04 다음 중 밑줄 친 것이 올바르지 <u>않은</u> 것을 고르세요.
① We get up early <u>in a morning</u>.
② The sun sets in <u>the west</u>.
③ Look at <u>the sky</u>.
④ Can you <u>bring</u> me the book?
⑤ There are a lot of <u>students</u> in the gym.

60

[05-06] 다음 중 우리말과 같도록 빈칸에 들어갈 알맞은 말을 고르세요.

05

I love watching the _____ leaves.

나는 형형색색의 나뭇잎들을 보는 것을 좋아한다.

① dark   ② many   ③ simple

④ beautiful   ⑤ colorful

06

Don't forget to _____ your umbrella when you go out.

외출할 때 우산 가져가는 것을 잊지 마라.

① get   ② catch   ③ take

④ bring   ⑤ give

07 다음 중 빈칸에 들어갈 알맞은 말을 고르세요.

It's cloudy.

There are a lot of dark _____ in the sky.

① sun   ② clouds   ③ rains

④ fog   ⑤ snow

08 다음 중 그림을 보고 빈칸에 들어갈 알맞은 말을 고르세요.

A rainbow is a(n) _____ of seven different colors.

① toy   ② cloud   ③ house

④ window   ⑤ arch

[09-10] 다음을 읽고 질문에 답하세요.

> Spring is warm.
>
> We can see a lot of flowers in spring.
>
> Summer is hot.
>
> We can swim in the sea.
>
> Fall is cool.
>
> We can see the colorful leaves in the mountains.
>
> Winter is cold.
>
> We can make a snowman in winter.

09 다음 중 이 글을 통해 알 수 <u>없는</u> 것을 고르세요.

① The weather is different during each season.

② It snows in winter.

③ Flowers bloom in spring.

④ We can see beautiful leaves in fall.

⑤ Summer begins in June.

10 다음 질문의 대답을 이 글에서 찾아 쓰세요.

> What's the weather like in spring?

11 다음 중 빈칸에 공통으로 들어갈 알맞은 말을 고르세요.

> · I think I'm catching a _____ .
>
> · I don't like winter because it's _____ .

① hot   ② snowy   ③ ball

④ cold   ⑤ chilly

12 다음 보기에서 빈칸에 들어갈 알맞을 말을 골라 쓰세요.

season	when	different

(1) We bought five _____ kind of cakes.

(2) We sometimes play football _____ it rains.

(3) My favorite _____ is summer.

13 다음 밑줄 친 부분을 바르게 고치세요.

Sam and I go swimming in <u>an</u> afternoon.

_____

14 다음 빈칸에 공통으로 들어갈 말을 쓰세요.

• There are many stars in the _____.
• There is a rainbow in the _____.

_____

15 다음 영어를 우리말로 쓰세요.

(1) A rainbow is a symbol of hope and happiness.

_____

(2) There are no clouds in the sky.

_____

WORD MASTER

TR 3-09-W

 다음 단어의 뜻을 쓰고, 단어를 세 번씩 더 써보세요.

01	**cloudy**	흐린	cloudy	cloudy	cloudy
02	**colorful**				
03	**different**				
04	**forget**				
05	**happiness**				
06	**hope**				
07	**leaf**				
08	**lucky**				
09	**mountain**				
10	**rainbow**				
11	**season**				
12	**snowman**				
13	**symbol**				
14	**weather**				
15	**year**				

Chapter 4

Pets

Her Best Friend

TR 3-10

Cindy has a dog.

Its name is Prince.

It has long, white fur and a short tail.

It wags its tail before her.

It likes to run and jump in the field.

It likes to chew on bones and meat.

It barks at strangers.

Cindy and Prince sometimes swim in the river together.

Prince is Cindy's best friend.

Cindy loves Prince a lot.

1 다음 문장이 이 글의 내용과 같으면 T에 동그라미를, 다르면 F에 동그라미 하세요.

(1) Cindy takes a walk with Prince every day.　　　T　　F

(2) Cindy sometimes eats meat.　　　T　　F

(3) Cindy and her dog swim in the river.　　　T　　F

2 다음 중에서 Cindy 앞에서 Prince가 하는 행동이 무엇인지 고르세요.

① swimming in the river　　② eating breakfast

③ feeding her dog　　④ walking her dog

⑤ wagging its tail

3 다음 중 Prince의 모습으로 언급하지 <u>않은</u> 것을 고르세요.

① 　　② 　　③

④ 　　⑤

4 다음 대화의 빈칸에 알맞은 말을 쓰세요.

> **A** What does Price do when it sees strangers?
> **B** It ＿＿＿＿＿＿＿＿＿＿＿＿＿ them.

WORDS

□ **fur** 털　□ **tail** 꼬리　□ **wag** 흔들다　□ **before** ~ 앞에(서)　□ **field** 들판　□ **chew** 씹다

□ **bone** 뼈　□ **meat** 고기　□ **bark** 짖다　□ **stranger** 낯선 사람　□ **together** 함께　□ **a lot** 많이

WORD CHECK

1 다음 단어와 그림을 연결하세요.

(1) 　　(2) 　　(3) 　　(4)

A. jump　　　B. field　　　C. bone　　　D. meat

2 다음 중 그림을 보고 빈칸에 들어갈 알맞은 말을 고르세요.

Paul _____ into the pool.

① barks　　　② jumps　　　③ swim
④ flies　　　⑤ walks

3 다음 우리말과 같도록 빈칸에 알맞은 단어를 골라 쓰세요.

(1) It has _____, white fur and a short tail. (long / middle)
그것은 긴 흰 털과 짧은 꼬리를 가지고 있다.

(2) It likes to run and jump in the _____. (gym / field)
그것은 들판에서 달리고 점프하는 것을 좋아한다.

(3) It _____ at strangers. (barks / runs)
그것은 낯선 사람들을 향해 짖는다.

GRAMMAR TIME

형용사의 어순

1 형용사는 명사 앞에 나와 명사를 꾸며줍니다.

This is a nice car. 이것은 멋진 자동차다.

형용사 명사

They are fresh vegetables. 그것들은 신선한 야채들이다.

형용사   명사

2 형용사가 한 개 이상일 때 다음의 순서로 씁니다.

숫자, 관사	크기	색깔	명사
the	large	white	building
a	small	brown	dog
three	big	yellow	buses

다음 보기에 주어진 단어들을 빈칸에 순서대로 쓰세요.

> **two**   **red**   **small**

(1) She is carrying _____ books.

> **small**   **a**   **black**

(2) I have _____ dog.

> **the**   **flowers**   **purple**

(3) Look at _____ .

TR 3-11

I have a pet cat.

Her name is Dotty.

She has black dots on her body.

She has lovely blue eyes.

She is friendly and she gets along with my pet dog Tommy.

She doesn't like bathing, but she loves being petted.

I feed her twice a day.

She likes to <u>have</u> milk, but her favorite is fish.

She sleeps in a small basket near my bed.

I love my pet cat very much.

1 다음 중 이 글의 내용과 <u>다른</u> 것을 고르세요.

① Dotty has blue eyes.　② Dotty likes to have fish.

③ Dotty sleeps with my dog.　④ My dog's name is Tommy.

⑤ Dotty has black dots on her body.

2 다음 중 밑줄 친 **have**와 같은 의미로 쓰인 문장을 고르세요.

① We don't <u>have</u> any water in the tank.

② We <u>have</u> lunch at noon.

③ She <u>has</u> three children.

④ Did you <u>have</u> a good time at the party?

⑤ Do you <u>have</u> brothers?

3 다음 중 Dotty가 싫어하는 것을 고르세요.

① 　② 　③

④ 　⑤

4 다음 대화의 빈칸에 알맞은 말을 쓰세요.

A How many times do you feed Dotty a day?

B I feed her _____.

WORDS

☐ **pet** 애완동물　☐ **name** 이름　☐ **dot** 점　☐ **body** 몸　☐ **lovely** 사랑스러운　☐ **friendly** 다정한

☐ **bath** 목욕하다　☐ **pet** (동물을) 쓰다듬다　☐ **feed** 먹이를 주다　☐ **twice** 두 번　☐ **fish** 물고기　☐ **near** 근처

1 다음 단어와 그림을 연결하세요.

(1)
(2)
(3)
(4)

A. black dots   B. bath   C. feed   D. basket

2 다음 중 우리말과 같도록 빈칸에 들어갈 알맞은 말을 고르세요.

> The dog has black _____ on its body.
> 그 개는 몸에 검은 점들이 있다.

① eyes   ② ears   ③ hair
④ nose   ⑤ dots

3 다음 우리말과 같도록 빈칸에 알맞은 단어를 골라 쓰세요.

(1) It has _____ blue eyes. (lovely / love)

그것은 사랑스러운 파란 눈을 가지고 있다.

(2) It doesn't like _____ . (bathing / sleeping)

그것은 목욕하는 것을 좋아하지 않는다.

(3) It sleeps in a small basket _____ my bed. (far / near)

그것은 내 침대 가까이 작은 바구니에서 잔다.

GRAMMAR TIME

형용사와 부사

1 명사에 -ly가 붙으면 형용사가 됩니다.

love → lovely	friend → friendly	week → weekly
사랑 사랑스러운	친구 친절한	주 매주의
cost → costly	time → timely	day → daily
비용 값비싼	시간 때맞춘	하루, 날 매일의

2 형용사에 -ly가 붙으면 부사가 됩니다. 부사는 동사, 형용사 등을 보충 설명해주는 역할을 합니다.

slow → slowly	real → really	careful → carefully
느린 느리게	진짜의 진짜, 정말로	주의 깊은 조심스럽게
kind → kindly	quick → quickly	happy → happily
친절한 친절하게	빠른 빠르게	행복한 행복하게
easy → easily	loud → loudly	wise → wisely
쉬운 쉽게	시끄러운 큰 소리로	현명한 현명하게

1 다음 괄호 안에서 알맞은 말을 고르세요.

(1) I can solve the problem (easy / easily).

(2) He drives (careful / carefully).

(3) They are (kind / kindly) to me.

(4) The boy is singing (loud / loudly).

(5) Tony is a (wise / wisely) boy.

(6) She has a (love / lovely) voice.

(7) This is not a (real / really) flower.

(8) My friends are very (friend / friendly).

UNIT 3 Fishbowl

🎧 TR 3-12

I have a small fishbowl in my room.

There is a fish named Kelly.

She is orange.

She has a beautiful tail.

At night, she sleeps in the hole of a rock.

She probably has some very pleasant dreams!

Kelly is a very greedy fish.

She never stops eating.

Her stomach looks like it is going to burst.

She has three friends.

All four of them live together happily in the fishbowl.

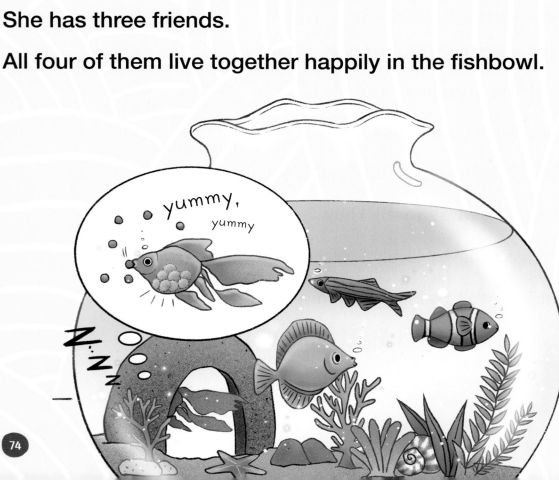

1 다음 중 이 글은 무엇에 관한 내용인지 고르세요.

① my favorite animals   ② going fishing with my Dad

③ the tail of fish   ④ a dream about fish

⑤ a fish in a fishbowl

2 다음 중 이 글의 내용과 <u>다른</u> 것을 고르세요.

① Kelly lives in a small fishbowl.   ② Kelly lives with other fish.

③ Kelly doesn't sleep at night.   ④ Kelly has a tail.

⑤ Kelly never stops eating.

3 다음 중 **Kelly**의 모습으로 가장 적절한 것을 고르세요.

①    ②    ③

④    ⑤

4 다음 대화의 빈칸에 알맞은 말을 쓰세요.

> **A** How many fish are there in the fishbowl?
>
> **B** There are _____ in the fishbowl.

WORDS

□ **fishbowl** 어항   □ **fish** 물고기(복수형도 fish)   □ **orange** 주황색   □ **hole** 구멍   □ **rock** 바위

□ **probably** 아마도   □ **pleasant** 즐거운   □ **dream** 꿈   □ **greedy** 욕심 많은   □ **never** 결코 ~ 아닌

□ **stomach** 위, 배   □ **burst** 터지다

1 다음 단어와 그림을 연결하세요.

(1) 　(2) 　(3) 　(4)

A. fishbowl　　B. oranges　　C. rock　　D. greedy

2 다음 중 빈칸에 들어갈 알맞은 말을 고르세요.

My _____ is to become a movie director.

① pet　　　　　　② friends　　　　　③ dream
④ name　　　　　⑤ room

3 다음 우리말과 같도록 빈칸에 알맞은 단어를 골라 쓰세요.

(1) At night, she sleeps in the hole of a _____. (rock / bed)
밤에 그녀는 바위의 구멍 안에서 잠을 잔다.

(2) She probably has some very _____ dreams! (pleasant / bad)
그녀는 아마도 매우 즐거운 꿈을 꾸는 거 같다!

(3) Her _____ looks like it is going to burst. (stomach / back)
그녀는 배가 터질 것처럼 보인다.

GRAMMAR TIME

some과 any의 의미와 쓰임

1 some은 '조금', '약간의', '몇몇의' 등의 의미를 가지고 있으며, 긍정문에 주로 쓰입니다.

2 some 다음에는 복수명사와 셀 수 없는 명사가 모두 올 수 있습니다.
I have **some** books. (o) 나는 몇몇의 책들이 있다. I have some book. (x)
I have **some** money. 나는 돈이 조금 있다.

3 부정문에는 some 대신 any를 사용합니다.
I don't have **any** books. 나는 책들이 조금도 없다.
I don't have **any** money. 나는 돈이 조금도 없다.

TIPS some과 any는 셀 수 없는 명사나 복수명사와 함께 쓰여 무엇의 양이나 수를 표현합니다.

---

1 다음 빈칸에 some이나 any를 쓰세요.

(1) She has ＿＿＿＿＿＿＿＿ water.

그녀는 물이 조금 있다.

(2) There are ＿＿＿＿＿＿＿＿ people in the park.

공원에 몇몇의 사람들이 있다.

(3) I don't have ＿＿＿＿＿＿＿＿ money in my wallet.

나의 지갑에 돈이 조금도 없다.

(4) I don't have ＿＿＿＿＿＿＿＿ more questions.

나는 더 할 질문이 조금도 없다.

(5) He doesn't have ＿＿＿＿＿＿＿＿ friends in Korea.

그는 한국에 친구들이 조금도 없다.

01 다음 중 짝지어진 관계가 <u>다른</u> 것을 고르세요.

① friend – friendly   ② slow – slowly

③ careful – carefully   ④ easy – easily

⑤ quick – quickly

[02-03] 다음 중 우리말과 같도록 빈칸에 들어갈 알맞은 말을 고르세요.

02

I can solve the problem _____.
나는 그 문제를 쉽게 풀 수 있다.

① really   ② wisely   ③ loudly

④ lovely   ⑤ easily

03

I don't have _____ money now.
나는 지금 돈이 조금도 없다.

① few   ② little   ③ a little

④ any   ⑤ some

04 다음 중 밑줄 친 것이 올바르지 <u>않은</u> 것을 고르세요.

① There are <u>some people</u> in the park.

② Alice is a <u>wise girl</u>.

③ My grandma <u>walks slowly</u>.

④ I have <u>small black a</u> dog.

⑤ Look at <u>the red flowers</u>.

[05-06] 다음 중 우리말과 같도록 빈칸에 들어갈 알맞은 말을 고르세요.

05
I _____ her twice a day.
나는 하루에 두 번 그녀에게 먹이를 준다.

① water   ② feed   ③ bath
④ pet   ⑤ walk

06
She _____ stops talking.
그녀는 결코 말하는 것을 멈추지 않는다.

① always   ② do   ③ will
④ never   ⑤ can

07 다음 중 빈칸에 공통으로 들어갈 말을 고르세요.

· The dog has long, black fur and a short _____ .
· The dog wags its _____ before her.

① tail   ② ear   ③ leg
④ eye   ⑤ body

08 다음 중 그림을 보고 빈칸에 들어갈 알맞은 말을 고르세요.

The dog _____ at strangers.

① barks   ② plays   ③ cuts
④ feeds   ⑤ bathes

> I have a small fishbowl in my room.
>
> There is a fish named Kelly.
>
> She is orange.
>
> She has a <u>beautiful</u> tail.
>
> At night, she sleeps in the hole of a rock.
>
> She probably has some very pleasant dreams!
>
> Kelly is a very greedy fish.
>
> She never stops eating.
>
> Her stomach looks like it is going to burst.
>
> She has three friends.
>
> All four of them live together _____ in the fishbowl.

09 다음 중 이 글을 통해 알 수 <u>없는</u> 것을 고르세요.

① Kelly의 몸 색상   ② Kelly가 자는 장소

③ 어항이 있는 장소   ④ Kelly가 좋아하는 음식

⑤ 어항의 물고기 수

10 다음 중 이 글의 빈칸에 들어갈 알맞은 말을 고르세요.

① really   ② happily   ③ friendly

④ carefully   ⑤ lovely

11 다음 중 이 글의 밑줄 친 **beautiful**의 반대말을 고르세요.

① pretty   ② dirty   ③ ugly

④ strong   ⑤ weak

12 다음 보기에서 빈칸에 들어갈 알맞을 말을 골라 쓰세요.

| basket | jump | meat |

(1) Vegetarians don't eat _____.   *vegetarian 채식주의자

(2) There are some oranges in the _____.

(3) The cat can _____ really high.

13 다음 보기에 주어진 단어들을 빈칸에 순서대로 쓰세요.

| yellow | three | pencils |

She has _____ _____ _____.

14 다음 밑줄 친 부분을 바르게 고치세요.

Don't eat too <u>quick</u>.

_____

15 다음 영어를 우리말로 쓰세요.

(1) She sleeps in a small basket near my bed.

_____

(2) My dog likes to chew on bones and meat.

_____

WORD MASTER

TR 3-12-W

 다음 단어의 뜻을 쓰고, 단어를 세 번씩 더 써보세요.

01	bark	짖다	bark	bark	bark
02	body				
03	chew				
04	dream				
05	field				
06	fishbowl				
07	friendly				
08	greedy				
09	meat				
10	pleasant				
11	probably				
12	stomach				
13	stranger				
14	together				
15	wag				

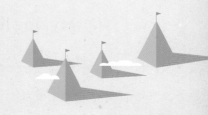

Chapter 5

In the Woods

There are so many <u>different</u> types of trees in the woods.

TR 3-13

Trees need sunlight and water to grow.

Trees are tall and strong.

Trees give us food like fruit and nuts.

Trees give birds a place to build their nests.

Trees give us shade.

Trees give us fresh air.

We can hear trees in the wind.

Trees are very useful to humans.

1 다음 중 이 글에서 언급하지 <u>않은</u> 내용을 고르세요.

① 숲에는 매우 다양한 나무들이 있다.

② 나무는 우리에게 먹을 것을 제공한다.

③ 나무는 새들에게 둥지를 만들 장소를 제공한다.

④ 나무는 인간에게 유용하다.

⑤ 나무는 우리에게 집을 지을 목재를 제공한다.

2 다음 중 빈칸에 들어갈 수 <u>없는</u> 것을 고르세요.

> Trees are useful to humans.
> They give us _____.

① shade   ② fresh air   ③ nuts

④ food   ⑤ sunlight

3 다음 중 밑줄 친 **different**와 반대되는 말을 고르세요.

① same   ② beautiful   ③ colorful

④ diligent   ⑤ tall

4 다음 대화의 빈칸에 알맞은 말을 쓰세요.

> **A** What do trees need to grow?
> **B** They need _____.

WORDS

□ **different** 다양한   □ **type** 종류   □ **woods** 숲   □ **grow** 자라다   □ **strong** 강한   □ **fruit** 과일

□ **nut** 견과   □ **build** 만들다   □ **nest** 둥지   □ **shade** 그늘   □ **fresh** 신선한   □ **air** 공기   □ **wind** 바람

□ **useful** 유용한   □ **human** 인간

1 다음 단어와 그림을 연결하세요.

(1) 　　(2) 　　(3) 　　(4)

A. nuts　　B. nest　　C. wind　　D. strong

2 다음 중 보기가 설명하는 것을 고르세요.

> This grows on a tree or bush.
> Its skin is thin or hard.
> Its insides are sweet and juicy.

① wind　　　② bird　　　③ fruit
④ water　　　⑤ vegetable

3 다음 우리말과 같도록 빈칸에 알맞은 단어를 골라 쓰세요.

(1) Trees need sunlight and water to _____. (grow / tall)
나무들은 성장하는 데 햇빛과 물이 필요하다.

(2) Trees give birds a _____ to build their nests. (place / time)
나무들은 새들에게 그들의 둥지를 만드는 장소를 제공한다.

(3) Trees are _____ to humans. (use / useful)
나무들은 인간에게 유용하다.

[명사＋ful] 형태의 형용사

1 명사에 -ful을 붙이면 형용사가 되어 뜻이 바뀝니다.

2 명사에 붙는 -ful은 '~이 가득한'이란 의미가 있습니다.

color (색, 색채)＋ful	→	colorful (다채로운) - 색이 풍부한
use (사용, 유용)＋ful	→	useful (유용한)
hope (희망)＋ful	→	hopeful (희망이 가득한)
power (힘)＋ful	→	powerful (힘이 센, 강력한)
beauty (미)＋ful	→	beautiful (아름다운)
help (도움)＋ful	→	helpful (도움이 되는)

1 다음 중 우리말과 같도록 빈칸에 들어갈 알맞은 말을 고르세요.

> Look at the _____ flowers in the picture.
> 사진 속의 알록달록한 꽃들을 봐라.

① colorful   ② powerful   ③ beautiful

④ useful   ⑤ hopeful

2 다음 괄호 안에서 알맞은 것을 고르세요.

(1) Her jump is very (power / powerful).

(2) Fire is a very (use / useful) tool.

(3) There is a (hope / hopeful) of his recovery.

Jimin and his family go camping.

They pack sleeping bags and a tent.

They love camping in the woods.

They find a campsite.

They set up a tent.

They make a campfire.

They cook food on the fire.

They eat dinner around the campfire.

They sleep in the tent at night.

Jimin likes sleeping in a tent with his family.

Camping in the woods is fun.

READING CHECK

1 다음 중 이 글이 무엇에 관한 내용인지 고르세요.

① field trip　　　　② making a campfire
③ cooking food on the fire　　④ setting up a tent
⑤ camping in the woods

2 다음 중 Jimin과 그의 가족이 하는 행동이 <u>아닌</u> 것을 고르세요.

① 　② 　③

④ 　⑤

3 다음 문장이 이 글의 내용과 같으면 T에 동그라미를, 다르면 F에 동그라미 하세요.

(1) Jimin likes sleeping in a tent with his family.　　T　　F

(2) Jimin doesn't cook food in the woods.　　T　　F

(3) Jimin's family likes camping in the woods.　　T　　F

4 다음 대화의 빈칸에 알맞은 말을 쓰세요.

A What does Jimin pack for camping?
B He packs _____.

WORDS

□ **camping** 캠핑, 야영　□ **pack** 짐을 싸다　□ **sleeping bag** 침낭　□ **woods** 숲　□ **campsite** 캠프장
□ **set up** 세우다　□ **tent** 텐트　□ **campfire** 캠프파이어　□ **around** ~ 주위에　□ **at night** 밤에

WORD CHECK

1 다음 단어와 그림을 연결하세요.

(1) 　　(2) 　　(3) 　　(4)

A. go camping　　B. set up a tent　　C. cook food　　D. campfire

2 다음 중 빈칸에 들어갈 알맞은 말을 고르세요.

> He sets up a _____ near the river.

① book　　　　② car　　　　③ dinner
④ tent　　　　⑤ wood

3 다음 우리말과 같도록 빈칸에 알맞은 단어를 골라 쓰세요.

(1) They love camping in the _____. (wood / woods)
그들은 숲에서 캠핑하는 것을 좋아한다.

(2) They eat dinner _____ the campfire. (around / on)
그들은 캠프파이어 주위에서 저녁식사를 한다.

(3) They sleep in the tent _____ night. (in / at)
그들은 밤에 텐트에서 잔다.

GRAMMAR TIME

[like/love+동사ing] 형태

1 동사 like나 love 다음에 [동사+ing]의 형태가 와서 '~하는 것을 좋아하다'라는 의미로 쓰입니다.

2 이때 [동사+ing]는 목적어 역할을 하는 동명사입니다.

I like **reading**. 나는 독서하는 것을 좋아한다.

They love **dancing**. 그들은 춤추는 것을 아주 좋아한다.

We like **listening** to the radio. 우리는 라디오 듣는 것을 좋아한다.

TIPS [동사+ing] 대신 [to+동사원형]을 사용할 수도 있습니다.

I like **cooking**. 나는 요리하는 것을 좋아한다.

= I like **to cook**.

1 다음 중 밑줄 친 단어의 역할이 <u>다른</u> 것을 고르세요.

① I like <u>reading</u>.

② They love <u>dancing</u>.

③ We like <u>listening</u> to radio.

④ She is <u>singing</u> on the stage.

⑤ She likes <u>cooking</u>.

2 다음 괄호 안에서 알맞은 것을 고르세요.

(1) They don't like (to sleeping / sleeping) in a tent.

(2) I like (watch / watching) movies.

(3) They love (eat / to eat) kimchi.

(4) He likes (reading / to reading) comic books.

UNIT 3 In the Woods

TR 3-15

Birds live in the woods.

They build their nests in trees.

Squirrels live in the woods.

They get their food from trees.

Rabbits live in the woods.

They eat grass, seeds, fruit, etc.

Butterflies live in the woods.

They eat plants or nectar from plants.

The woods give shelters and food to animals and insects.

The woods are home to animals and insects.

1 다음 중 이 글의 내용과 <u>다른</u> 것을 고르세요.

① 새들은 나무에 둥지를 만든다.　② 다람쥐들은 숲에 산다.

③ 토끼들은 풀과 과일 등을 먹는다.　④ 숲은 곤충들에게 살 장소를 제공한다.

⑤ 나비들은 나뭇잎만 먹고 산다.

2 다음 중 이 글에서 언급하지 <u>않은</u> 것을 고르세요.

① 　② 　③

④ 　⑤

3 다음 이 글의 밑줄 친 **They**가 의미하는 것을 쓰세요.

_____

4 다음 대화의 빈칸에 알맞은 말을 쓰세요.

> **A** Where do squirrels get their food?
>
> **B** They get their food _____ .

WORDS
- **woods** 숲　□ **nest** 둥지　□ **squirrel** 다람쥐　□ **rabbit** 토끼　□ **seed** 씨앗　□ **fruit** 과일
- **etc.** 등등　□ **butterfly** 나비　□ **plant** 식물　□ **nectar** 즙, 꿀　□ **shelter** 안식처　□ **insect** 곤충

1 다음 단어와 그림을 연결하세요.

(1)  (2)  (3)  (4)

· · · ·

· · · ·

A. squirrel   B. seeds   C. insects   D. butterfly

2 다음 보기의 This가 설명하는 것을 고르세요.

> This is an insect.
> This has colorful wings and a thin body.

① bird   ② butterfly   ③ spider
④ squirrel   ⑤ horse

3 다음 우리말과 같도록 빈칸에 알맞은 단어를 골라 쓰세요.

(1) They _____ their food from trees. (get / buy)
그들은 나무에서 음식을 얻는다.

(2) They eat grass, _____, fruit, etc. (plants / seeds)
그들은 풀, 씨앗, 과일 등을 먹는다.

(3) The woods give _____ and food to animals. (shelters / tents)
숲은 동물들에게 안식처와 음식을 제공한다.

GRAMMAR TIME

전치사 from과 to의 의미와 쓰임

1 전치사 from은 '～에서 온', '～에게서', '～부터'라는 의미로 출발점 또는 출처를 나타냅니다.

She's **from** Canada. 그녀는 캐나다 출신이다.

This is a letter **from** my mom. 이것은 엄마에게서 온 편지다.

Rain comes **from** clouds. 비는 구름에서 내린다.

2 전치사 to는 '～에게'라는 의미로 어떤 것을 받는 대상을 나타내거나, '～로', '～쪽으로'라는 방향을 나타냅니다.

He gave it **to** his sister. 그는 그것을 여동생[누나]에게 주었다.

He walked **to** the office. 그는 사무실로 걸어갔다.

---

1 다음 우리말과 같도록 괄호 안에서 알맞은 것을 고르세요.

(1) He's going (to / from) Paris.

그는 파리로 갈 것이다.

(2) She got it (to / from) her friend.

그녀는 그것을 친구한테서 받았다.

(3) Turn (to / from) the left at the next corner.

다음 모퉁이에서 왼쪽으로 돌아라.

2 다음 우리말과 같도록 빈칸에 공통으로 들어갈 말을 쓰세요.

A Where are you _____ ? 어디에서 왔니?

B I'm _____ Korea. 한국에서 왔어.

[01-03] 다음 중 빈칸에 들어갈 알맞은 말을 고르세요.

01

They are _____ Canada.

① with   ② at   ③ from
④ to   ⑤ for

02

We like _____ to the radio.

① listen   ② listening   ③ listens
④ to listening   ⑤ to listens

03

He gave his gloves _____ his sister.

① in   ② at   ③ from
④ to   ⑤ for

04 다음 중 밑줄 친 단어의 역할이 <u>다른</u> 것을 고르세요.

① I like <u>playing</u> computer games.

② They are <u>dancing</u> on stage.

③ We like <u>listening</u> to the radio.

④ She likes <u>singing</u>.

⑤ My dad loves <u>cooking</u>.

[05-06] 다음 중 우리말과 같도록 빈칸에 들어갈 알맞은 말을 고르세요.

05
This car is very _____.

이 자동차는 매우 힘이 좋다.

① hopeful   ② colorful   ③ careful
④ useful   ⑤ powerful

06
The woods give _____ and food to animals.

숲은 동물들에게 안식처나 음식을 제공한다.

① stages   ② sunlight   ③ buildings
④ trees   ⑤ shelters

07 다음 중 빈칸에 들어갈 알맞은 말을 고르세요.

Trees give us shade.

Trees give us fresh air.

Trees are _____ to humans.

① hopeful   ② colorful   ③ careful
④ useful   ⑤ powerful

08 다음 중 그림을 보고 빈칸에 들어갈 알맞은 말을 고르세요.

They _____ a tent.

① take care of   ② work out
③ put on   ④ set up
⑤ wake up

[09-11] 다음을 읽고 질문에 답하세요.

The tree is a tall plant.

The tree has a hard trunk, branches, and leaves.

Trees need sunlight and water to grow.

Trees give us food like fruits and nuts.

Trees give birds a place to build their nests.

Trees give us oxygen.

Trees are very _____ to humans and animals.

*oxygen 산소 / human 인간

09 다음 중 이 글에 언급하지 <u>않은</u> 것을 고르세요.

① 나무의 모양 ② 나무가 성장하기 위해 필요한 것

③ 나무가 종류가 많은 이유 ④ 나무가 인간에게 제공하는 것

⑤ 나무가 새들에게 제공하는 것

10 다음 중 이 글의 빈칸에 들어갈 알맞은 말을 고르세요.

① lovely ② important ③ difficult

④ enough ⑤ beautiful

11 다음 중 보기의 This가 설명하는 것을 고르세요.

· This is a gas with no color.

· This exists in the air.

*exist 존재하다

① dust ② oxygen ③ pollution

④ plant ⑤ water

12 다음 보기에서 빈칸에 들어갈 알맞은 말을 골라 쓰세요.

| insects | get | around |

(1) I'm going to walk _____ the lake.

(2) Can I _____ something to eat?

(3) Most _____ love flowers.

13 다음 우리말과 같도록 빈칸에 알맞은 말을 쓰세요.

This is a letter _____ my mom.
이것은 엄마에게서 온 편지다.

_____

14 다음 주어진 단어를 이용하여 빈칸에 알맞은 말을 쓰세요.

Ted also likes _____ English. (learn)

_____

15 다음 영어를 우리말로 쓰세요.

(1) The woods are home to animals and insects.

_____

(2) Jimin likes sleeping in a tent with his family.

_____

🎈 다음 단어의 뜻을 쓰고, 단어를 세 번씩 더 써보세요.

01 **air**	공기	air	air	air
02 **butterfly**				
03 **fresh**				
04 **grow**				
05 **human**				
06 **insect**				
07 **nest**				
08 **plant**				
09 **rabbit**				
10 **seed**				
11 **shade**				
12 **shelter**				
13 **strong**				
14 **useful**				
15 **woods**				

Chapter 6

Health

TR 3-16

Mike washes his hands before meals.

He brushes his teeth after meals.

He always brushes his teeth before he goes to bed.

Lydia eats breakfast every day.

She doesn't skip meals.

She likes to eat vegetables and fruit.

She doesn't eat salty food.

Sam plays football or baseball after school.

He likes playing outdoor sports.

He is active all the time.

He works out regularly.

1 다음 문장이 이 글의 내용과 같으면 T에 동그라미를, 다르면 F에 동그라미 하세요.

(1) Mike brushes his teeth before he goes to bed.   T   F

(2) Sometimes Lydia skips lunch.   T   F

(3) Sam likes playing baseball.   T   F

2 다음 중 이 글에서 건강한 습관으로 언급하지 <u>않은</u> 것을 고르세요.

① 손 씻기   ② 아침식사 하기   ③ 이 닦기

④ 운동하기   ⑤ 일찍 일어나기

3 다음 각자의 모습에 줄을 연결하세요.

(1) Mike   (2) Lydia   (3) Sam

A.   B.   C.

4 다음 대화의 빈칸에 알맞은 말을 쓰세요.

A What does Mike do before meals?

B He _____ before meals.

WORDS

□ **wash** 씻다, 닦다   □ **meal** 식사   □ **always** 항상   □ **breakfast** 아침식사   □ **every day** 매일

□ **skip** 거르다   □ **vegetable** 야채   □ **fruit** 과일   □ **salty** 짠   □ **football** 미식축구   □ **outdoor** 야외의

□ **active** 활동적인   □ **work out** 운동하다   □ **regularly** 규칙적으로

1 다음 단어와 그림을 연결하세요.

(1)

(2)

(3)

(4)

A. vegetables   B. skip meals   C. play baseball   D. work out

2 다음 중 빈칸에 들어갈 알맞은 말을 고르세요.

> _____ are plants such as cabbages, potatoes, and onions.

① Animals   ② Fruits   ③ Vegetables

④ Flowers   ⑤ Meals

3 다음 우리말과 같도록 빈칸에 알맞은 단어를 골라 쓰세요.

(1) She doesn't _____ meals. (skip / stop)
그녀는 식사를 거르지 않는다.

(2) She doesn't eat _____ food. (salt / salty)
그녀는 짠 음식을 먹지 않는다.

(3) He is _____ all the time. (active / action)
그는 항상 활동적이다.

GRAMMAR TIME

명사의 복수형

1 대부분의 명사에 -s 또는 -es를 붙여 명사의 복수형을 만듭니다.
boy → boys   bus → buses

2 그러나 일부 명사들은 -s 또는 -es를 붙여 명사의 복수형을 만들 수 없습니다.
이러한 명사들은 반드시 알아두어야 합니다.

불규칙적으로 변하는 명사	man 남자 → men 남자들 woman 여자 → women 여자들 foot 발 → feet 발들 child 아이 → children 아이들 mouse 쥐 → mice 쥐들 tooth 이 → teeth 이들

1 다음 괄호 안에서 알맞은 것을 고르세요.

(1) There are five (woman / women) in the cafe.

(2) The baby has two (tooth / teeth).

(3) How many (childs / children) do you have?

(4) There is a (boy / boys) in the classroom.

(5) The man is chasing a (mouse / mice).

(6) There are only three (man / men) in the restaurant.

TR 3-17

There is a sofa in the living room.

The sofa is my dad's favorite thing.

My dad spends hours sitting on the sofa watching TV.

He also likes sleeping on the sofa.

The _____ is like a bed for him.

My dad doesn't do anything during the weekends.

He's getting fatter and fatter.

I am worried about his health.

I think he needs to exercise.

What should I do for him?

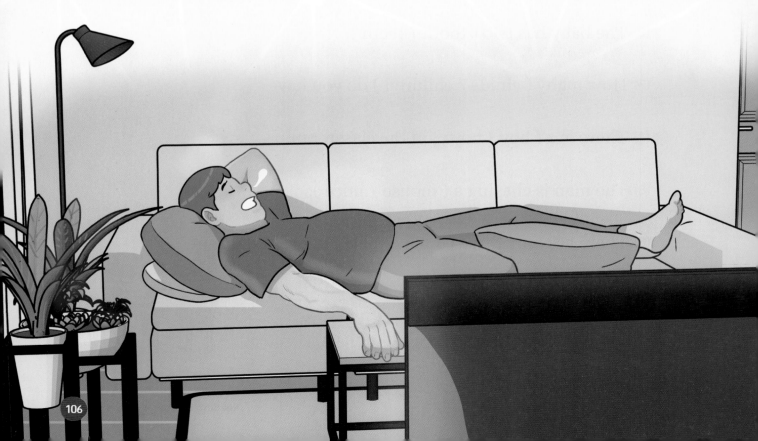

1 다음 문장이 이 글의 내용과 같으면 T에 동그라미를, 다르면 F에 동그라미 하세요.

(1) My dad is very busy during the weekends.   T   F

(2) My dad spends hours reading books every day.   T   F

(3) My dad doesn't sleep on the sofa.   T   F

2 다음 중 빈칸에 들어갈 알맞은 말을 고르세요.

① TV   ② sofa   ③ dad

④ bed   ⑤ living room

3 다음 중 글쓴이가 아빠에게 바라는 것을 고르세요.

①    ②    ③

④   ⑤

4 다음 대화의 빈칸에 알맞은 말을 쓰세요.

> **A** Why is Ted worried about his dad's health?
>
> **B** His dad _____.

WORDS

□ **thing** 것   □ **spend** (시간을) 보내다   □ **hour** 시간   □ **be like** ~과 같다   □ **anything** (부정문) 아무것도

□ **during** ~ 동안   □ **weekend** 주말   □ **fat** 뚱뚱한   □ **need** 필요하다   □ **exercise** 운동하다, 운동

WORD CHECK

1 다음 단어와 그림을 연결하세요.

(1) 　(2) 　(3) 　(4)

A. living room　B. sofa　C. fat　D. exercise

2 다음 중 빈칸에 들어갈 알맞은 말을 고르세요.

> I play basketball with my friends _____.

① in 2001　　② last week　　③ yesterday
④ on the weekends　　⑤ last Sunday

3 다음 우리말과 같도록 빈칸에 알맞은 단어를 골라 쓰세요.

(1) My dad doesn't do _____ during the weekends.
아빠는 주말 동안 아무것도 하지 않는다.　　(nothing / anything)

(2) I am _____ about his health. (worried / sorry)
나는 그의 건강이 걱정된다.

(3) I think he needs to _____. (exercise / excuse)
나는 그가 운동이 필요하다고 생각한다.

GRAMMAR TIME

형용사의 비교급

1. 사물의 모양이나 상태를 설명하는 말이 형용사입니다.
   사물을 '더 ~하다'라고 다른 사물과 비교할 때 [형용사+er] 형태의 비교급을 씁니다.
   Your bag is small. 너의 가방은 작다.
   My bag is smaller. 나의 가방이 더 작다.

2. 두 개의 사물을 비교할 때는 [형용사+er than]을 씁니다.
   My bag is smaller than your bag. 나의 가방이 네 가방보다 더 작다.

3. [get(grow, become)+비교급+and+비교급]은 '점점 더 ~해지다'라는 의미입니다.
   It's getting warmer and warmer. 날씨가 점점 더 더워지고 있다.
   It's getting smaller and smaller. 그것은 점점 더 작아지고 있다.

---

1 다음 우리말과 같도록 보기의 단어를 이용하여 빈칸에 알맞을 말을 쓰세요.

old	thick	small	light

(1) I'm _____ than Tom.
   나는 톰보다 나이다 더 많다.

(2) The computer is _____ than my bag.
   그 컴퓨터가 내 가방보다 더 가볍다.

(3) My dog is _____ than the cat.
   내 개가 그 고양이보다 더 작다.

(4) My book is _____ than yours.
   내 책이 너의 것보다 더 두껍다.

---

2 다음 주어진 단어들을 우리말과 같도록 배열하세요.

Alice가 Kelly보다 키다 더 크다. (Kelly / is / than / taller)

Alice _____.

Good Habits for Our Health

🎧 TR 3-18

Here are 10 healthy daily habits.

Healthy habits can help you improve your physical and mental well-being.

01   Brush your teeth after meals.

02   Don't eat too much <u>junk food</u>.

03   Wash your hands before meals.

04   Get enough sleep.

05   Drink enough water every day.

06   Spend time with your friends.

07   Exercise regularly.

08   Don't listen to loud music.

09   Wear a helmet when you ride a bike.

10   Maintain a healthy weight.

1 다음 중 밑줄 친 <u>junk food</u> 대신 쓸 수 있는 말을 고르세요.

① healthy diet   ② fast food   ③ Chinese food

④ cold food   ⑤ good food

2 다음 중 healthy daily habits으로 언급하지 <u>않은</u> 것을 고르세요.

①    ②   ③

④   ⑤

3 다음 중 그림과 관련된 습관을 고르세요.

① Get enough sleep.

② Drink enough water every day.

③ Exercise regularly.

④ Don't listen to loud music.

⑤ Maintain a healthy weight.

4 다음 대화의 빈칸에 알맞은 말을 쓰세요.

A   What do you have to do before meals?

B   We have to _____.

WORDS

□ **healthy** 건강한   □ **habit** 습관   □ **improve** 향상시키다   □ **physical** 육체의   □ **mental** 정신의

□ **well-being** 행복   □ **enough** 충분한   □ **exercise** 운동하다   □ **regularly** 규칙적으로

□ **loud** 시끄러운   □ **maintain** 유지하다   □ **weight** 몸무게

WORD CHECK

1 다음 단어와 그림을 연결하세요.

(1) 　　(2) 　　(3) 　　(4)

A. loud music　　B. ride a bike　　C. weight　　D. friends

2 다음 중 보기의 **This**가 설명하는 것을 고르세요.

- We need this when we play baseball or ride a bike.
- This protects our head.
- This is made of plastic.

① 　② 　③ 　④ 　⑤

3 다음 우리말과 같도록 빈칸에 알맞은 단어를 골라 쓰세요.

(1) Get _____ sleep. (enough / some)

충분한 잠을 자라.

(2) Spend time _____ your friends. (on / with)

친구들과 시간을 보내라.

(3) _____ a healthy weight. (Maintain / Put)

건강한 몸무게를 유지하라.

GRAMMAR TIME

when의 의미와 쓰임

1 when은 접속사 역할을 하여 '(~하는) 때에', '~하면' 등의 의미를 가지고 있습니다.

   <u>I read books</u> **when** <u>I'm free</u>. 나는 한가로울 때 책을 읽는다.
   　　문장　　　　　　　　문장

   TIPS 접속사는 단어와 단어 그리고 문장과 문장을 연결하는 역할을 합니다.

2 when은 의문문에 쓰여 '언제'라는 의미를 가지고 있습니다. 이때 when은 접속사가 아니라 부사로 쓰이고 있습니다. When으로 질문하면 Yes나 No로 대답할 수 없습니다.

   A: When are you going to visit Korea? 너는 한국을 언제 방문할 거니?
   B: Next week. 다음 주.

---

1 다음 중 **when**의 쓰임이 <u>다른</u> 것을 고르세요.

① Please call me <u>when</u> you get home.

② <u>When</u> do you usually have dinner?

③ Wear a helmet <u>when</u> you ride a bike.

④ Close your eyes <u>when</u> you want to sleep.

⑤ <u>When</u> you cross the street, look out for cars.

---

2 다음 영어를 우리말로 쓰세요.

(1) Be careful when you use scissors.

　　_____

(2) When do you have lunch?

　　_____

01 다음 중 복수형이 올바르지 <u>않은</u> 것을 고르세요.

① man – men   ② foot – foots   ③ child – children

④ bus – buses   ⑤ mouse – mice

02 다음 중 빈칸에 알맞지 <u>않은</u> 말을 고르세요.

> My bag is _____ than your bag.

① light   ② heavier   ③ bigger

④ smaller   ⑤ cheaper

03 다음 중 대화의 빈칸에 들어갈 알맞은 말을 고르세요.

> **A** _____ are you going to marry him?
> **B** Next year.

① Who   ② Do   ③ Does

④ Where   ⑤ When

04 다음 중 **when**의 쓰임이 <u>다른</u> 것을 고르세요.

① Please call me <u>when</u> you are free.

② <u>When</u> do you eat breakfast?

③ Wear a seatbelt <u>when</u> you drive.

④ Drink hot milk <u>when</u> you want to sleep.

⑤ He wants to be a pilot <u>when</u> he grows up.

[05-06] 다음 중 우리말과 같도록 빈칸에 들어갈 알맞은 말을 고르세요.

05

> Drink _____ water every day.
> 매일 충분한 물을 마셔라.

① short ② clean ③ healthy
④ enough ⑤ regular

06

> I am _____ about his health.
> 나는 그의 건강이 걱정된다.

① worried ② think ③ carful
④ favorite ⑤ full

07 다음 중 빈칸에 들어갈 알맞은 말을 고르세요.

> My dad is getting fatter and fatter. I think he needs to _____.

① read books ② make dinner
③ lose weight ④ take a break
⑤ buy a car

08 다음 중 그림과 일치하도록 빈칸에 들어갈 알맞은 말을 고르세요.

> She _____ regularly.

① takes a walk ② works out
③ takes a break ④ goes to bed
⑤ wakes up

[09-11] 다음을 읽고 질문에 답하세요.

> Here are 7 healthy daily habits.
>
> 01 Don't skip meals.
>
> 02 Brush your teeth after meals.
>
> 03 Sleep 7 to 8 hours every night.
>
> 04 Drink enough water every day.
>
> 05 Exercise _____.
>
> 06 Wear a helmet when you ride a bike.
>
> 07 Eat vegetables and fruit.

09 다음 중 이 글에서 언급하지 <u>않은</u> 것을 고르세요.

① 식사 후 이를 닦아라.　　　② 잠을 충분히 자라.

③ 충분한 물을 마셔라.　　　④ 야채와 과일을 먹어라.

⑤ 일찍 일어나라.

10 다음 중 보기의 내용과 의미가 유사한 것을 고르세요.

> Don't skip meals.

① Eat breakfast.

② Get enough sleep.

③ Get up early in the morning.

④ Maintain a healthy weight.

⑤ Brush your teeth after meals.

11 다음 중 이 글의 빈칸에 들어갈 알맞은 말을 고르세요.

① lovely　　　② regularly　　　③ friendly

④ never　　　⑤ sometimes

12 다음 보기에서 빈칸에 들어갈 알맞을 말을 골라 쓰세요.

health	weekend	active

(1) Milk is good for our _____.

(2) He's 80 years old, but he is still very _____.

(3) Have a good _____.

13 다음 밑줄 친 곳을 바르게 고치세요.

> There are five <u>man</u> in the cafe.

_____

14 다음 우리말과 같도록 주어진 단어를 이용하여 빈칸에 공통으로 알맞은 말을 쓰세요.

> It is getting _____ and _____. (warm)
> 날씨가 점점 더 따뜻해지고 있다.

_____

15 다음 영어를 우리말로 쓰세요.

(1) She doesn't eat salty food.

_____

(2) My dad doesn't do anything during the weekends.

_____

WORD MASTER

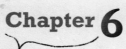

TR 3-18-W

 다음 단어의 뜻을 쓰고, 단어를 세 번씩 더 써보세요.

01	**active**	활동적인	active	active	active
02	**always**				
03	**enough**				
04	**habit**				
05	**healthy**				
06	**improve**				
07	**maintain**				
08	**meal**				
09	**mental**				
10	**outdoor**				
11	**physical**				
12	**regularly**				
13	**salty**				
14	**weekend**				
15	**weight**				

Memo

Memo

Longman

Reading

Mentor

joy

START 3

WORKBOOK

Reading Mentor joy START 3

WORKBOOK

1 다음 보기에서 의미와 일치하는 단어를 고르고 세 번 쓰세요.

| uniform | blue | pants | suit | bank | wear |

01 바지 _____ _____ _____

02 정장, 양복 _____ _____ _____

03 입다 _____ _____ _____

04 은행 _____ _____ _____

05 유니폼 _____ _____ _____

06 파란(색) _____ _____ _____

2 다음 중 우리말과 같도록 빈칸에 들어갈 알맞은 말을 고르세요.

01

He looks _____ in a suit.
그는 정장이 잘 어울린다.

① old ② sad ③ nice ④ happy ⑤ cold

02

My mom _____ at a bank.
나의 엄마는 은행에서 일한다.

① walks ② works ③ has ④ plays ⑤ studies

3 다음 영어와 우리말을 연결하세요.

01 a blue shirt   •   • ⓐ 넥타이를 매다

02 wear a tie   •   • ⓑ 파란 셔츠

03 a school uniform •   • ⓒ 교복

4 다음 괄호 안에서 알맞은 것을 고르세요.

01 We go to school every (day / days).

02 (Every people / Everyone) arrived on time.

03 We go camping every (year / years).

5 다음 영어를 우리말로 쓰세요.

01 He wears a suit to work every day.

    → _____

02 My mom looks good in her uniform.

    → _____

1 다음 보기에서 의미와 일치하는 단어를 고르고 세 번 쓰세요.

| pool | fast | bike | carefully | drive | glasses |

01 안경 _____ _____ _____

02 운전하다 _____ _____ _____

03 수영장 _____ _____ _____

04 빠르게 _____ _____ _____

05 자전거 _____ _____ _____

06 조심스럽게 _____ _____ _____

2 다음 중 우리말과 같도록 빈칸에 들어갈 알맞은 말을 고르세요.

01

She _____ swim very fast.

그녀는 매우 빠르게 수영할 수 있다.

① will ② can ③ do ④ is ⑤ is going to

02

My grandmother is _____ glasses.

나의 할머니는 안경을 쓰고 있다.

① doing ② riding ③ wearing ④ driving ⑤ reading

3 다음 영어와 우리말을 연결하세요.

01 a swimming suit • 　　　　　• ⓐ 안전벨트를 매다

02 ride a bike • 　　　　　　• ⓑ 수영복

03 wear a seatbelt • 　　　　• ⓒ 자전거를 타다

4 다음 우리말과 같도록 밑줄 친 부분을 바르게 고치세요.

01 Sam isn't <u>take</u> a shower. → _____
샘은 샤워를 하고 있지 않다.

02 Kevin isn't <u>read</u> a book now. → _____
케빈은 지금 책을 읽고 있지 않다.

03 My friends <u>is</u> not playing outside. → _____
내 친구들은 바깥에서 놀고 있지 않다.

04 The boy is not <u>eat</u> pizza. → _____
그 소년은 피자를 먹고 있지 않다.

5 다음 영어를 우리말로 쓰세요.

01 She enjoys riding a bike.

→ _____

02 He drives carefully.

→ _____

1 다음 보기에서 의미와 일치하는 단어를 고르고 세 번 쓰세요.

> comfortable   cool   blue jeans   need   hot   someday

01 언젠가 _____ _____ _____

02 멋진 _____ _____ _____

03 편안한 _____ _____ _____

04 더운 _____ _____ _____

05 필요하다 _____ _____ _____

06 청바지 _____ _____ _____

2 다음 중 우리말과 같도록 빈칸에 들어갈 알맞은 말을 고르세요.

01

There is a school _____ on the shirt.

셔츠에는 학교 로고가 있다.

① map   ② picture   ③ uniform   ④ bag   ⑤ logo

02

He _____ to wear a coat someday.

그는 언젠가 코트를 입기를 바란다.

① tells   ② hopes   ③ needs   ④ does   ⑤ can

3 다음 영어와 우리말을 연결하세요.

01 go out •   • ⓐ 검은 반바지

02 all year round •   • ⓑ 1년 내내

03 black shorts •   • ⓒ 외출하다

4 다음 우리말과 같도록 밑줄 친 부분을 바르게 고치세요.

01 Sam is wearing blue <u>pant</u>.   → _____
   샘은 파란색 바지를 입고 있다.

02 I want to buy two pairs of <u>sock</u>.   → _____
   나는 양말 2켤레를 사고 싶다.

03 I cut my finger with the <u>scissor</u>.   → _____
   나는 가위에 손이 베었다.

5 다음 영어를 우리말로 쓰세요.

01 He wears blue jeans when he goes out.

   → _____

02 It is very hot all year round in Indonesia.

   → _____

1 다음 보기에서 의미와 일치하는 단어를 고르고 세 번 쓰세요.

throw	pitcher	helmet	catch	miss	fly

01 투수 _____ _____ _____

02 날아가다 _____ _____ _____

03 놓치다 _____ _____ _____

04 잡다 _____ _____ _____

05 헬멧 _____ _____ _____

06 던지다 _____ _____ _____

2 다음 중 우리말과 같도록 빈칸에 들어갈 알맞은 말을 고르세요.

01

Ted is playing baseball _____ his friends.

테드는 친구들과 야구를 하고 있다.

① with　　② on　　③ in　　④ to　　⑤ beside

02

He tries to _____ the ball with the bat.

그는 방망이로 공을 치려고 한다.

① want　　② hit　　③ catch　　④ buy　　⑤ throw

3 다음 영어와 우리말을 연결하세요.

01 throw a ball   •   • ⓐ 공을 놓치다

02 catch a ball   •   • ⓑ 공을 잡다

03 miss a ball   •   • ⓒ 공을 던지다

4 다음 현재진행형을 의문문으로 쓰세요.

01 You are listening to music.

→ _____

02 He is playing basketball.

→ _____

03 They are watching TV.

→ _____

5 다음 영어를 우리말로 쓰세요.

01 His job is to catch the ball with his glove.

→ _____

02 James hits the ball and the ball is flying to Tom.

→ _____

1 다음 보기에서 의미와 일치하는 단어를 고르고 세 번 쓰세요.

soccer	referee	sit	blow	shoes	whistle

01 호루라기 _____ _____ _____

02 불다 _____ _____ _____

03 앉다 _____ _____ _____

04 심판 _____ _____ _____

05 축구 _____ _____ _____

06 신발 _____ _____ _____

2 다음 중 우리말과 같도록 빈칸에 들어갈 알맞은 말을 고르세요.

01

He can _____ his hands.

그는 손을 사용할 수 있다.

① give　　② buy　　③ take　　④ sit　　⑤ use

02

We are not _____ at soccer.

우리는 축구를 잘하지 못한다.

① hungry　　② fast　　③ bad　　④ good　　⑤ well

3 다음 영어와 우리말을 연결하세요.

01 grab the ball   •   • ⓐ 호루라기를 불다

02 blow the whistle •   • ⓑ 공을 잡다

03 favorite sport   •   • ⓒ 좋아하는 운동

4 다음 문장을 부정문으로 바꾸세요.

01 My dad is reading a book.

→ _____

02 They are my friends.

→ _____

03 We were busy yesterday.

→ _____

5 다음 영어를 우리말로 쓰세요.

01 Cathy and I are sitting in the stands.

→ _____

02 Steve grabs the ball with his hands.

→ _____

1 다음 보기에서 의미와 일치하는 단어를 고르고 세 번 쓰세요.

> bring   enter   direction   animal   ladder   rule

01 규칙 _____ _____ _____

02 들어가다 _____ _____ _____

03 가져오다 _____ _____ _____

04 지시 _____ _____ _____

05 사다리 _____ _____ _____

06 동물 _____ _____ _____

2 다음 중 우리말과 같도록 빈칸에 들어갈 알맞은 말을 고르세요.

01

Always _____ the lifeguard's directions.
항상 안전요원의 지시를 따라라.

① bring   ② use   ③ enter   ④ follow   ⑤ say

02

Don't _____ into the swimming pool.
수영장으로 다이빙하지 마라.

① eat   ② do   ③ follow   ④ dive   ⑤ run

3 다음 영어와 우리말을 연결하세요.

01 take a shower   •   • ⓐ 수영장 주변

02 a swimming pool •   • ⓑ 샤워하다

03 a pool area   •   • ⓒ 수영장

4 다음 괄호 안에서 알맞은 것을 고르세요.

01 We (don't / doesn't) drink coffee.

02 My dad (don't / doesn't) have a car.

03 I (don't / doesn't) play computer games.

04 (Don't / Doesn't) make a noise.

05 Don't (be / is) angry with her.

5 다음 영어를 우리말로 쓰세요.

01 Don't bring animals into the pool area.

→ _____

02 Do warm-ups before entering the swimming pool.

→ _____

1 다음 보기에서 의미와 일치하는 단어를 고르고 세 번 쓰세요.

| season | summer | warm | cool | colorful | mountain |

01 여름 _____ _____ _____

02 시원한 _____ _____ _____

03 따뜻한 _____ _____ _____

04 산 _____ _____ _____

05 형형색색의 _____ _____ _____

06 계절 _____ _____ _____

2 다음 중 우리말과 같도록 빈칸에 들어갈 알맞은 말을 고르세요.

01

We can see _____ flowers in spring.

우리는 봄에 많은 꽃들을 볼 수 있다.

① a lot of   ② so   ③ much   ④ too   ⑤ very

02

We can _____ a snowman in winter.

우리는 겨울에 눈사람을 만들 수 있다.

① play   ② see   ③ make   ④ do   ⑤ sell

14

3 다음 영어와 우리말을 연결하세요.

01 four seasons ·

02 colorful leaves ·

03 your favorite season ·

· ⓐ 형형색색의 나뭇잎들

· ⓑ 네가 좋아하는 계절

· ⓒ 4계절

4 다음 괄호 안에서 알맞은 것을 고르세요.

01 There are many (flower / flowers) in the garden.

02 I have (a lot of / much) coins.

03 There is (a lot of / many) milk in the bucket.

04 We don't have (a lot of / many) money.

5 다음 영어를 우리말로 쓰세요.

01 There are four seasons in a year.

→ _____

02 We can swim in the sea.

→ _____

1 다음 보기에서 의미와 일치하는 단어를 고르고 세 번 쓰세요.

sunny cloud dark forget fall umbrella

01 구름 _____ _____ _____

02 떨어지다 _____ _____ _____

03 우산 _____ _____ _____

04 어두운 _____ _____ _____

05 잊다 _____ _____ _____

06 맑은 _____ _____ _____

2 다음 중 우리말과 같도록 빈칸에 들어갈 알맞은 말을 고르세요.

01

There are _____ clouds in the sky.
하늘에는 구름 한 점 없다.

① many ② much ③ too ④ no ⑤ so

02

I _____ an umbrella today.
나는 오늘 우산이 필요하다.

① need ② take ③ buy ④ give ⑤ come

3 다음 영어와 우리말을 연결하세요.

01 take your umbrella •

• ⓐ 맑은 날씨

02 sunny weather •

• ⓑ 우산을 가져가다

03 dark clouds •

• ⓒ 먹구름

4 다음 우리말과 같도록 빈칸에 take나 bring을 쓰세요.

01 Can you _____ me a glass of water?
물 한 잔 가져와 주시겠어요?

02 Don't forget to _____ your homework tomorrow.
내일 숙제 가져오는 거 잊지 마라.

03 Can you _____ this and put it away?
이거 가져가서 치워줄 수 있나요?

04 Don't forget to _____ your umbrella.
잊지 말고 우산을 가져가라.

5 다음 영어를 우리말로 쓰세요.

01 The rain is falling from the sky.

→ _____

02 I love making a snowman with my friends.

→ _____

1 다음 보기에서 의미와 일치하는 단어를 고르고 세 번 쓰세요.

| rainbow   circle   hope   lucky   different   green |

01 희망 _____ _____ _____

02 원 _____ _____ _____

03 행운의 _____ _____ _____

04 초록색 _____ _____ _____

05 다른 _____ _____ _____

06 무지개 _____ _____ _____

2 다음 중 우리말과 같도록 빈칸에 들어갈 알맞은 말을 고르세요.

01

A rainbow is actually _____ like a circle.
실제로 무지개는 원처럼 둥근 모양이다.

① shape   ② round   ③ symbol   ④ star   ⑤ square

02

The colors of the rainbow look _____ beautiful.
무지개의 색은 매우 아름답다.

① many   ② very   ③ too   ④ much   ⑤ only

3 다음 영어와 우리말을 연결하세요.

01 a symbol of the rainbow •

02 seven different colors •

03 half of the rainbow •

• ⓐ 무지개의 절반

• ⓑ 무지개의 상징

• ⓒ 7개의 다른 색들

4 다음 밑줄 친 부분을 바르게 고치세요.

01 The sun rises in a west. → _____

02 She can play a piano very well. → _____

03 What do you usually do in an evening? → _____

5 다음 영어를 우리말로 쓰세요.

01 We can only see half of the rainbow.

→ _____

02 A rainbow is a symbol of hope and happiness.

→ _____

1

다음 보기에서 의미와 일치하는 단어를 고르고 세 번 쓰세요.

fur	field	river	chew	meat	bark

01 들판 _____ _____ _____

02 씹다 _____ _____ _____

03 고기 _____ _____ _____

04 강 _____ _____ _____

05 짖다 _____ _____ _____

06 털 _____ _____ _____

2

다음 중 우리말과 같도록 빈칸에 들어갈 알맞은 말을 고르세요.

01

Prince _____ its tail before her.

프린스는 그녀 앞에서 꼬리를 흔든다.

① gets   ② cries   ③ puts   ④ works   ⑤ wags

02

Prince barks at _____ .

프린스는 낯선 사람들에게 짖는다.

① friends   ② people   ③ dogs   ④ strangers   ⑤ family

3 다음 영어와 우리말을 연결하세요.

01 a short tail •

02 run in the field •

03 swim in the river •

• ⓐ 들판에서 달리다

• ⓑ 강에서 수영하다

• ⓒ 짧은 꼬리

4 다음 주어진 단어를 바르게 배열하여 빈칸에 쓰세요.

01 She wants to buy a _____. (black / big / car)

02 I have_____ cat. (small / a / white)

03 Look at the_____. (balloons / red)

5 다음 영어를 우리말로 쓰세요.

01 Prince likes to chew on bones and meat.

→ _____

02 Prince has long, white fur and a short tail.

→ _____

1 다음 보기에서 의미와 일치하는 단어를 고르고 세 번 쓰세요.

> lovely   dot   blue   twice   basket   sleep

01 점 _____ _____ _____

02 사랑스러운 _____ _____ _____

03 잠자다 _____ _____ _____

04 바구니 _____ _____ _____

05 2번 _____ _____ _____

06 파란(색) _____ _____ _____

2 다음 중 우리말과 같도록 빈칸에 들어갈 알맞은 말을 고르세요.

01

It sleeps in a small basket _____ my bed.
그것은 내 침대 가까이에 있는 작은 바구니에서 잔다.

① far   ② near   ③ on   ④ under   ⑤ over

02

I love my pet cat very _____.
나는 나의 애완 고양이를 아주 많이 사랑한다.

① well   ② many   ③ good   ④ fast   ⑤ much

3 다음 영어와 우리말을 연결하세요.

01 get along with   •

02 lovely blue eyes   •

03 a pet cat   •

• ⓐ 사랑스러운 파란 눈

• ⓑ 애완 고양이

• ⓒ ~와 잘 지내다

4 다음 우리말과 같도록 괄호 안에서 알맞은 것을 고르세요.

01 He walks (quick / quickly).
그는 빠르게 걷는다.

02 He (real / really) likes you.
그는 너를 정말 좋아한다.

03 He spoke in a (loud / loudly) voice.
그가 큰 목소리로 말했다.

04 She has a (love / lovely) voice.
그녀는 아름다운 목소리를 가지고 있다.

5 다음 영어를 우리말로 쓰세요.

01 Dotty doesn't like bathing, but she loves being petted.

→ _____

02 Dotty likes to have milk, but her favorite is fish.

→ _____

1 다음 보기에서 의미와 일치하는 단어를 고르고 세 번 쓰세요.

> fish   tail   pleasant   greedy   stomach   together

01 함께 _____ _____ _____

02 배 _____ _____ _____

03 즐거운 _____ _____ _____

04 물고기 _____ _____ _____

05 꼬리 _____ _____ _____

06 욕심 많은 _____ _____ _____

2 다음 중 우리말과 같도록 빈칸에 들어갈 알맞은 말을 고르세요.

01

I have a small _____ in my room.

나는 내 방에 작은 어항을 가지고 있다.

① fish   ② fishbowl   ③ friend   ④ stomach   ⑤ bed

02

Kelly _____ stops eating.

켈리는 결코 먹는 것을 멈추지 않는다.

① often   ② don't   ③ will   ④ never   ⑤ isn't

3 다음 영어와 우리말을 연결하세요.

01 live together • • ⓐ 매우 욕심 많은 물고기

02 a very greedy fish • • ⓑ 함께 살다

03 have pleasant dreams • • ⓒ 즐거운 꿈을 꾸다

4 다음 빈칸에 some이나 any를 쓰세요.

01 She has _____ coins.

02 There are _____ cucumbers in the basket.

03 They don't have _____ free time.

04 He doesn't have _____ special plans.

5 다음 영어를 우리말로 쓰세요.

01 At night, Kelly sleeps in the hole of a rock.

→ _____

02 Her stomach looks like it is going to burst.

→ _____

1 다음 보기에서 의미와 일치하는 단어를 고르고 세 번 쓰세요.

different grow place bird shade human

01 성장하다 _____ _____ _____

02 장소 _____ _____ _____

03 다른 _____ _____ _____

04 새 _____ _____ _____

05 인간 _____ _____ _____

06 그늘 _____ _____ _____

2 다음 중 우리말과 같도록 빈칸에 들어갈 알맞은 말을 고르세요.

01

Trees need _____ and water to grow.
나무들은 자라기 위해서 햇빛과 물이 필요하다.

① sunny　　② rain　　③ sunlight　　④ food　　⑤ air

02

We can hear trees in the _____.
우리는 바람에서 나무들의 소리를 들을 수 있다.

① fruit　　② sun　　③ food　　④ woods　　⑤ wind

3 다음 영어와 우리말을 연결하세요.

01 build nests   •　　　　　• ⓐ 인간에게 유용한

02 fresh air   •　　　　　• ⓑ 신선한 공기

03 useful to humans •　　　　　• ⓒ 둥지를 만들다

4 다음 우리말과 같도록 보기에서 빈칸에 들어갈 알맞은 말을 골라 쓰세요.

colorful	powerful	hopeful

01 The garden is full of _____ flowers.
그 정원은 다채로운 꽃들로 가득 차 있다.

02 The patient's situation is not very _____.
그 환자의 상황이 희망적이지 못하다.

03 Korea will be a more _____ country in the world.
한국은 세계에서 더 강력한 나라가 될 것이다.

5 다음 영어를 우리말로 쓰세요.

01 There are so many different types of trees in the woods.

→ _____

02 Trees give us food like fruit and nuts.

→ _____

1 다음 보기에서 의미와 일치하는 단어를 고르고 세 번 쓰세요.

find   cook   pack   woods   tent   bag

01 짐을 싸다 _____ _____ _____

02 숲 _____ _____ _____

03 텐트 _____ _____ _____

04 발견하다 _____ _____ _____

05 가방 _____ _____ _____

06 요리하다 _____ _____ _____

2 다음 중 우리말과 같도록 빈칸에 들어갈 알맞은 말을 고르세요.

01

They pack _____ bags and a tent.
그들은 침낭과 텐트를 꾸린다.

① walking   ② eating   ③ sleeping   ④ running   ⑤ cooking

02

They sleep in the tent at _____.
그들은 밤에 텐트에서 잔다.

① night   ② day   ③ noon   ④ evening   ⑤ woods

3 다음 영어와 우리말을 연결하세요.

01 set up a tent   •   • ⓐ 캠프파이어 주변에

02 around the campfire •   • ⓑ 캠프파이어를 만들다

03 make a campfire   •   • ⓒ 텐트를 치다

4 다음 주어진 단어를 이용하여 빈칸에 알맞은 말을 쓰세요.

01 I like _____. (read)

02 They love _____. (dance)

03 We like _____ to radio. (listen)

04 She likes _____. (cook)

5 다음 영어를 우리말로 쓰세요.

01 Jimin likes sleeping in a tent with his family.

→ _____

02 They love camping in the woods.

→ _____

1 다음 보기에서 의미와 일치하는 단어를 고르고 세 번 쓰세요.

> build   squirrel   rabbit   seed   butterfly   insect

01 곤충 _____   _____   _____

02 다람쥐 _____   _____   _____

03 만들다, 짓다 _____   _____   _____

04 나비 _____   _____   _____

05 씨앗 _____   _____   _____

06 토끼 _____   _____   _____

2 다음 중 우리말과 같도록 빈칸에 들어갈 알맞은 말을 고르세요.

01

> They _____ their food from the trees.
> 그들은 나무에서 음식을 얻는다.

① eat   ② want   ③ get   ④ love   ⑤ give

02

> The woods are _____ to animals and insects.
> 숲은 동물들과 곤충들의 집이다.

① grass   ② sun   ③ home   ④ plants   ⑤ woods

3 다음 영어와 우리말을 연결하세요.

01 live in the woods •

02 eat plants •

03 shelters and food •

• ⓐ 숲에서 살다

• ⓑ 안식처와 음식

• ⓒ 식물을 먹다

4 다음 우리말과 같도록 괄호 안에서 알맞은 것을 고르세요.

01 This is a letter (to / from) my mom.
이것은 엄마에게서 온 편지다.

02 They are (to / from) Canada.
그들은 캐나다 출신이다.

03 I gave my computer (to / from) Sam.
나는 컴퓨터를 샘에게 주었다.

04 They went (to / from) the park yesterday.
그들은 어제 공원에 갔다.

5 다음 영어를 우리말로 쓰세요.

01 They eat plants or nectar from plants.

→ _____

02 They eat grass, seeds, fruits, etc.

→ _____

1 다음 보기에서 의미와 일치하는 단어를 고르고 세 번 쓰세요.

salty active vegetable football outdoor meal

01 식사 _____ _____ _____

02 야채 _____ _____ _____

03 미식축구 _____ _____ _____

04 야외의 _____ _____ _____

05 짠 _____ _____ _____

06 활동적인 _____ _____ _____

2 다음 중 우리말과 같도록 빈칸에 들어갈 알맞은 말을 고르세요.

01

She doesn't _____ meals.

그녀는 식사를 거르지 않는다.

① skip ② play ③ brush ④ eat ⑤ love

02

He works out _____.

그는 규칙적으로 운동한다.

① every week ② regularly ③ often
④ sometimes ⑤ never

3 다음 영어와 우리말을 연결하세요.

01 eat salty food   •

02 all the time   •

03 outdoor sports   •

• ⓐ 야외 스포츠

• ⓑ 항상

• ⓒ 짠 음식을 먹다

4 다음 괄호 안에서 알맞은 것을 고르세요.

01 There are 5 (childs / children) in the room.

02 There are only 3 (woman / women) in the store.

03 How many (tooth / teeth) does the dog have?

04 Wash your hands and (foot / feet) when you get home.

5 다음 영어를 우리말로 쓰세요.

01 He brushes his teeth after meals.

→ _____

02 He likes playing outdoor sports.

→ _____

1 다음 보기에서 의미와 일치하는 단어를 고르고 세 번 쓰세요.

weekend	fat	exercise	think	health	potato

01 건강 _____ _____ _____

02 주말 _____ _____ _____

03 뚱뚱한 _____ _____ _____

04 운동하다 _____ _____ _____

05 감자 _____ _____ _____

06 생각하다 _____ _____ _____

2 다음 중 우리말과 같도록 빈칸에 들어갈 알맞은 말을 고르세요.

01

There is a sofa in the _____.

거실에는 소파가 하나 있다.

① home   ② living room   ③ house
④ room   ⑤ classroom

02

He also likes _____ on the sofa.

그는 또한 소파에서 자는 것을 좋아한다.

① eating   ② talking   ③ sleeping   ④ spending   ⑤ working

3 다음 영어와 우리말을 연결하세요.

01 worry about   •   • ⓐ 주말 동안

02 during the weekends •   • ⓑ ~을 걱정하다

03 sit on the sofa   •   • ⓒ 소파에 앉다

4 다음 우리말과 같도록 주어진 단어를 이용하여 빈칸에 알맞을 말을 쓰세요.

01 Sam is _____ than Tom. (fast)
샘은 톰보다 더 빠르다.

02 He is _____ than my dad. (tall)
그는 나의 아빠보다 키가 더 크다.

03 My house is _____ than her house. (small)
나의 집은 그녀의 집보다 더 작다.

5 다음 영어를 우리말로 쓰세요.

01 My dad doesn't do anything during the weekends.

→ _____

02 I think he needs to exercise.

→ _____

1 다음 보기에서 의미와 일치하는 단어를 고르고 세 번 쓰세요.

habit mental enough loud healthy weight

01 습관 _____ _____ _____

02 건강한 _____ _____ _____

03 시끄러운 _____ _____ _____

04 몸무게 _____ _____ _____

05 충분한 _____ _____ _____

06 정신의 _____ _____ _____

2 다음 중 우리말과 같도록 빈칸에 들어갈 알맞은 말을 고르세요.

01

Don't eat too _____ junk food.

정크푸드를 너무 많이 먹지 마라.

① so   ② much   ③ enough   ④ many   ⑤ high

02

Don't _____ to loud music.

시끄러운 음악을 듣지 마라.

① watch   ② sing   ③ study   ④ listen   ⑤ read

3 다음 영어와 우리말을 연결하세요.

01 physical wellbeing •   • ⓐ 자전거를 타다

02 ride a bike •   • ⓑ 건강한 몸무게

03 healthy weigh •   • ⓒ 육체적 행복

4 다음 중 when의 쓰임이 <u>다른</u> 것을 고르세요.

① Please call me <u>when</u> you see her.

② <u>When</u> I was young, I lived in Korea.

③ He reads books <u>when</u> he's free.

④ Be careful <u>when</u> you cross the street.

⑤ <u>When</u> did you see her?

5 다음 영어를 우리말로 쓰세요.

01 Healthy habits can help you improve your mental well-being.

   → _____

02 Wear a helmet when you ride a bike.

   → _____

Memo

Memo

Memo

WORKBOOK